T0130122

Also by Thomas Richard Harry

The Delicate Illusion

The Gathering of the Clan

BOOM! A Revolting Situation

GOD

Versus

THE IDEA OF GOD

Divinity is what we think,
Faith is what we experience

by
Thomas Richard Harry

BALBOA.
PRESS
A DIVISION OF HAY HOUSE

Balboa Press books may be ordered through booksellers or by contacting:

Balboa Press
A Division of Hay House
1663 Liberty Drive
Bloomington, IN 47403
www.balboapress.com
1 (877) 407-4847

Print information available on the last page.

ISBN: 978-1-5043-8656-2 (sc)
ISBN: 978-1-5043-8658-6 (hc)
ISBN: 978-1-5043-8657-9 (e)

Library of Congress Control Number: 2017913183

Balboa Press rev. date: 10/11/2017

NIV
The New International Version (NIV) Study Bible
(Grand Rapids Zondervan Bible Publishers 1985).

"Any God I ever felt in church I brought in with me. And I think all the other folks did too. They come to church to *share* God not find God."

Alice Walker, Author of *The Color Purple*

Table of Contents

Prologue

God and Me, A Shaky Relationship at Best

Heavens no, despite its title, this is not really a book about God—how could it be? It's about the present-day, Judeo-Christian portrayal and depiction of God, to at least this questioning writer, by the reformed version of the Western Christian Church, i.e., mainline American Protestantism. That's the branch with which I'm most acquainted. Even more narrowly, this is writing reflecting my personal experience in pursuit of assured belief in its modern day depiction of the Divine, and some comforting degree of faith in support of such belief.

So, who cares? Well, the fact that you're reading this indicates at least a degree of curiosity, if nothing else. It's a highly personal issue that most of us ponder in the quiet of our own thoughts at different and various times throughout our journeys through life. Theologian Karl Barth (1886-1968) once suggested that the most pressing question people ask when hearing a sermon is: "Is it true?"[1] That equates to doubt. As a Christian I find this troubling. For the Church it should be reason to pause and reflect on what it preaches today, and that is my message here.

To reiterate, this is not strictly speaking a scholarly undertaking. It should not be understood as being more than an experienced and mature layman's informed analysis and personal conclusions in pursuit of truth, or at least of understanding.[2] It reflects my personal experience in seeking to believe in and be in a relationship with God, as and in the manner taught by this branch of Western Christianity today. In some sense either I or the Church can be judged a failure, for doubt continues strong within me. You may be the judge in deciding the value, or lack thereof, for you of what I have concluded for myself.

What I've concluded is spelled out in some detail in the chapters that follow. In a nutshell, it is that what is real, what is unquestionable in religious pursuit, and has been throughout history, is the idea of the Divine. Whether or not the god of the idea actually exists, is real (as we understand the term "real"), we probably can never know. And that doesn't appear to be the most important feature of belief for mankind. What is important is the value, the utility, of the idea. By utility I mean usefulness, perhaps even necessity: the principle and end of utilitarian ethics, meaning that which is conducive to the happiness and well-being of the greatest number of people. For whom? For us earth-bound mortals. That seems ultimately the purpose of the idea of God. Support for us, enduring what for many is a fragile and uncomfortable existence in the here and now. I trust what I have to share will be meaningful.

So, here goes.

After years of church attendance, a fair amount of study, a great deal of reflection, consideration, and self-doubt, I don't think I really believe in God. At least not in the evolved vision and presentation of the biblical God of Western Christianity today. It has taken me a long, (long) time to come out and face that conclusion. It's acceptable today to express skepticism—just why I'm not sure—but not outright disbelief. I've hunkered down behind the cloak of skepticism for years. Now seems time to shed it. While taking this overt action may invite criticism, even ostracism, fortunately today no longer burning at the stake (Hallelujah!).

How did I arrive at this realization? I asked myself two rather straightforward questions. The first was one of credence:

If an infinite and perfect God (by definition) exists outside of time (history)—always has, does and always will—while finite mankind exists in time (history) how can there be any intercourse or relationship or even awareness between the two? Thus, for us finites,

God—assuming God—must be unknown, even unknowable. To God as presented we must be, if anything, but a blink of an eye; poof!

Well, what about the Church's historical presentation of Jesus of Nazareth? What about it? People have been worshiping gods, and the God of the Hebrew Bible for some time prior to his appearance in the public domain, and since. For the Christian Church, Jesus, the Christ, represents God active in history. It's their solution to how we can know God. For the Church, Jesus—declared fully human and fully God by this institution—is the necessary "bridge" connecting the finite to the infinite. For many it's a persuasive argument; for what appears to be a growing number it seems to fall short. We will take up this serious Jesus-God relationship in depth in Chapter Seven. It is of course an important—critical—subject within Christianity. But here it's a subsidiary aspect of the central question, the conundrum, of God vs. the idea of God.

We are thinking creatures who have learned to conceptualize. That is, we have the intellectual power of forming notions, ideas or concepts. And we can imagine, i.e., we can form a mental image of something (an idea or notion) not actually present to the senses. This allows for conjuring up "abstracts," or abstractions. These are ideas we mentally form which exist only as representations of something we can know by our senses or by our understanding (what it means to me). Examples include: beauty, good, perfection, justice, patriotism, etc. These are objective abstract notions which we humans can only know and/or appreciate subjectively (individually, as we understand it, appreciate it and/or value it).

The highest objective idea of the good is the notion man has of God, as defined. But for man to hold this idea of God is to imagine the perfect; there is nothing comparable, again by definition. How is the imperfect to comprehend the perfect? The human answer is through the revealed word of this perfect aseity, what we refer to as God. For Christians and Jews this word is believed to be delivered by the Hebrew and Christian Bibles respectively. Therein, God appears upon occasion to act in time (history) but no place else.

This revealed word advises us that at the beginning, man and

God were in perfect harmony; the Master and his creation(s) were in perfect rapport until man (in immaturity, or ignorance) fell from grace and harmony with God. Religion, ever since, has been struggling to get mankind to repent and live in accord with the dictates of God, as presented by religion. By so doing, the original harmony with and between God and man would be restored, for the purported benefit of humanity.

Since biblical times, this seems a never-ending drama between two worlds, our material world and God's purported heavenly world. The material vs. the immaterial; the imperfect vs. the perfect, the seen vs. the unseen. Such a scenario seems to me, today, to be seriously contrived, fictitious. We can in our minds easily construct an idea of God from the idea of the perfect. But that perfection is only an idea. It's an abstract. It is not something that is "real" in our material or mortal sense, except to the degree that we, individually, subjectively, make it real, i.e., believe in it and have faith (confidence) in it.

That was my first question. How under the preached circumstances can there be any relationship between me and God, be I a Christian or of some other faith? Christians will (should) immediately respond, "Jesus is the answer to your question." I understand, but would ask that you defer shouting out the party line until we have had the opportunity to hear a bit more about what I have to share with you here. Hang in there; allow me the benefit of doubt at this point.

The second question I asked myself was, "What is the purpose of God?" at least from man's viewpoint—the "why" of God? If God has no functional purpose, is only a representation of the good, then why worship it? If God does have a discernible purpose, what does this encompass and mean for humankind? I'm convinced that biblical revelation does offer an answer to this, and I'll share it with you (Moses seems to have figured this out a long time ago). I doubt you will be surprised by the revelations but might well be with my conclusion.

So how did I get to this position, this personal religiously dubious state of mind?

I was raised nominally as a Christian Scientist. From junior high school onward both my religious training and exposure was for all intents and purposes non-existent. My religious void continued into young adulthood. If I saw the inside of a church—any church—during those years, I cannot now recall it. Still, if asked, I would refer to myself as a Christian, non-denominational, but a Christian. In the year of our Lord 1968, I married. My wonderful new wife, unlike me, was a baptized and pretty regularly church-attending Christian young lady. After we were married, however, church attendance was sporadic.

After a number of years living and working abroad our family, now including three young sons, relocated back to the Midwest and shortly thereafter began attending a Presbyterian church near our home. As it happened, a new Pastor was called the same year we arrived, and I was fortunate to spend the next almost twenty years as a regular part of his congregation. I say "I" inasmuch as my wife Connie passed away in 1987. But in any event, I had the experience of belonging to a church. I must mention that during those years, I was not a member (I had never been baptized). Connie had been the member. Following a subsequent remarriage, my second wife, Susan, was. Nonetheless, I felt it was "my church." Whatever the nature of my Christianity, it was both accepted there and sufficient for the purpose, if not explored by myself too deeply or too much effort made to develop it.

Circumstances once again made me a widower. Following her valiant multi-year struggle, Connie had succumbed to the effects of cancer at the far too young age of 44. Susan similarly passed away from cancer following thirteen years of marriage; she at only 61. During all this, "my pastor," Dr. Robert Dowland, had been through this with me. I can't say I used the church, or Bob, as a crutch, but it was comforting to have someone on a personal basis and the church on an institutional basis to look to during these joint tragedies.

Well, under the heading "life's unpredictability," mine was again about to undergo an unanticipated tectonic shift. Under circumstances almost too unbelievable to relate—and so I won't—shortly after Susan's death I was reacquainted with a widowed "previous love" I had not seen or heard from for 43 years. We had been sweethearts in high school and during my years in college.

Talk about serendipity, fate or destiny, whatever you might wish to attribute it (invisible hands?), it happened: two individuals at loose ends once again in the autumn of their lives. One in Missouri; one in California; both with common memories and perhaps even a deeply dormant common affection that despite the span of almost half a century had never totally eclipsed. After a period of several months corresponding they decided to meet, and did so in the spring of 2003; they continued corresponding, met again in August, October and November. They decided it was not too late to try again for marriage. On February 14, 2004 (yes, Valentine's Day!), they finally exchanged vows, with the grown children of both, and even friends from the earlier years, attending them. (Wow!)

Just what does all this personal biographical detail have to do with my shaky relationship with God? Good and understandable question. Let me see if I can satisfactorily answer it.

As it happens, my wife Linda's adult background is of a strong conservative evangelical nature. As such, our religious backgrounds are distinct, to say the least. Over these past thirteen years it has been my pleasure to accompany her to Sunday services regularly at her church of choice, which at the time of our marriage was Baptist. Several years ago now we began attending a rather conservative Presbyterian church where we both are members currently. Needless to say, this has been a turn of religious exposure I previously had not experienced.

At any rate, such devotional attendance has provided me with an interest more penetrating, more questioning towards the Christian faith than I have ever previously experienced. It has, I must say, been a positive one overall; one that has made me look at and consider Christianity on a much deeper, broader and more personal basis than ever before. It has made me realize that I have mostly believed superficially. With this realization, I have for the past several years devoted considerable time "bringing myself up to speed." What has been the result of all this church attendance, self-searching, sectarian study and education? Unfortunately, it is not one of a greater faith, but one of a greater skepticism.

The pious 11th century Archbishop of Canterbury St. Anselm declared, "I believe in order to understand." Unbelievers, Anselm taught, "Strive to understand but never can because they do not believe, for in religion faith plays the part played by experience in the understanding of the things of the world."[3] This may well be the case, but in my mind I first must understand if I am to accept, to believe. Some contend that faith and belief are separate achievements. They may be. For the purpose at hand, I accept that belief is based not on fact, but on faith; that disbelief is based not on fact but on lack of faith. For me the issue here is about the truth-of rather than of faith-in.

And so the search goes on. For Linda, my striving is perplexing. There is no issue here for her; she and St. Anselm are of a common mind: she believes, and that's sufficient; that's truth. I plod on, perhaps in a never-ending journey like in Samuel Beckett's cryptic play, *"Waiting for Godot"*: ever hopeful, never fulfilled. I think that's why I have finally given up the chase.

But giving up the chase, so to speak, does not necessarily preclude having God, or more certainly the idea of God, in your life. I have concluded that life as we have come to know it and live it is abetted and nurtured by the utility of this idea of God. I firmly believe in it, and it is about this that I write here. The idea of God does not mean one necessarily automatically believes in the god of the idea, only that one is aware of it. Even atheists are, by necessity, aware of the god of the idea.

Chapter One

A Steep Hill to Climb

*"Only one thing is certain - - that is nothing is certain.
If this statement is true, it is also false."*
-Ancient Paradox

Thesis: Yes, there is a God.

Antithesis: No, there is no God.

Synthesis: After a very prolonged period, nothing yet.

Where do your thoughts fall on this scale of belief? Is there, isn't there or what else might there be? Perhaps what follows will shed some light on this long-debated issue. Maybe not. In any event, for many the search for belief can be a steep hill to climb.

When I use the term "God" I mean what the Church teaches, a divinity considered the Supreme Being, the creator and ruler of the universe; something numinous and transcendental. Something well beyond man's untrained ability to imagine. I do not mean a deified person or object. Such Supreme Being has historically assumed various forms, expressions, or characteristics for various peoples in various cultures. It has been pointed out that every culture develops its own idea of God.

Why does man believe in, or need to be taught to believe in, God? There are good and demonstrable reasons why, and we will delve into them. They explain just why we believe, or at least try and believe, in such a Supreme Being. It's really a matter of self-interest.

So, while rationally we do not know the does or does not of God itself, there is demonstrably a rational (does exist) idea of God (Chapter Five). There is also a rational purpose (does exist) for the god of that idea (Chapter Six), and a questionably rational institution, the Church, (Chapters Three and Four) which defends and promotes its version of the god of the idea. We will explore this idea of God in depth here as I have come to hold that it is this idea itself as opposed to its subject that defines what it is we hold as belief. I have also come to the conclusion that God, as Christian mankind holds it in its subjective and collective mind as the result of the idea (belief), is both a reality and more importantly a human necessity. As someone has famously said, if God didn't exist, we would have to invent it. That's a provocatively interesting statement, and one we will pick up again.

I believe strongly in the concept of God. However, whether or not there is a god, independent of the idea, rationally we have yet to figure out how to either demonstrate this, or to finally refute it. In this sense we are all non-corroborated agnostics, no matter what we might believe, or the degree of confidence (faith) we have in that belief. We start here from that position; we don't know.

What we do know, religiously speaking, we learn from the Church. The Church in turn relies on the Bible, the received word of God, for its teaching. For centuries, this chain of knowledge was both stable and authoritative. Then, the apparent results of what we today call science began to cast doubt on biblical "truths." This was and is a challenge for the Church.

In the case of scientific conclusions vs. religious beliefs (reason vs. faith), don't let anyone fool you: Western religion and science have since classical Hellenistic times been at odds on significant worldly matters. This is not a new issue. While that may not come as news to most, both cannot be right in their opposing conclusions. Under the law of contradiction two opposing propositions cannot both be true. One of them has it wrong. Which is the best horse to bet on here, the seen or the unseen? That might depend upon the context of their positions.

Western religions—Christianity for purposes here—have for

centuries been playing defense as the physical, and lately even the social sciences have progressively demonstrated pragmatic concepts of knowledge and understandings of worldly matters. These not infrequently differ sharply from the revealed religious presentation of those same events as described in the Judeo-Christian Bible. Our world and the heavens most probably weren't made in six days of spiritually creative activity. Earth most likely isn't about 4,004 years old—more like 4.5 to 4.6 billion years, give or take a hundred million years, according to science—and man as we know him today most probably didn't appear on earth fully human in one day, no assembly required. From a historical scholarly viewpoint, it seems highly improbable that the first century Jewish charismatic eschatological preacher, Jesus of Nazareth, was a god, or "God," in the divine Christian sense of the word. He was so anointed well after the fact by a minority of Church elders who looked to him as their religious inspiration and raison d ètre. Admittedly this was done, as we might say, in an evolving and generally good faith way. We'll go into these matters more in the pages to come, citing specifics where the Church has attempted to reconcile these differences within its own teachings.

Religion (the Church) is built and sustained upon faithful belief in the unseen by the revealed divine word of its God, the Bible. It has no other authentic evidence or source to quote. To have the biblical word of God questioned is to challenge the basis of religion itself. God, as presented by the Church, is a powerful conceptual as well as practical influence on man. But the historical presentation of God by the Church has problems associated with it, exacerbated by the accumulated findings of science. On the other hand, as Lord Jonathan Sacks (Former chief rabbi of the United Hebrew Congregations of the British Commonwealth) pointed out, "No society has survived for long without either a religion or a substitute for religion." Many, many on this third rock from the sun take monotheistic religion as a given. Should we? Belief in a religion is a conviction based on a matter of faith, which represents trust. How far can/should this be taken in matters of a worldly nature?

As a product of my time I favor rational verified explanations of worldly matters based upon evidence sufficient to be accepted as truth by a reasonable person. I consider such explanations organic, and evolutionary. That is, as knowledge expands and accumulates, explanations are fine-tuned to represent the best and most current evidence and thinking, or modified or discarded as and if new evidence disproves the earlier understanding. Under this hypothesis, nothing is definitive—even for science—but everything we currently believe we know about worldly matters is subject to change if and as necessary. This is how mankind has slowly experienced worldly progress over the past few thousand years in spite of spiritual claims often to the contrary. It has only been in relatively recent times (see below) that such biblical claims have been challenged, and in the minds of not just a few, questioned or discredited.

Some call this thought process materialistic. Materialism is simply a philosophical theory. It regards matter and its motions as constituting the universe. All phenomena, including those of the mind, are considered as due to material agencies and without spiritual implications. The alternative to this philosophy is one of Biblicism which holds that the Judeo-Christian Bible provides the truth about our material world and its inhabitants. At its most conservative, it relies exclusively and literally upon what the Bible says about worldly issues.

The basis for my choice of philosophies is experience, not mine personally but the history of Western man. For almost two millennia (from about 300 BCE to about 1500 CE), the dominant institution in non-oriental developed societies was the Church. It was in the main the exclusive institution of learning and repository of knowledge, libraries for example, during this period. People were taught, if taught they were, and learned what the Church wanted them to learn, which was a God-based curriculum focused upon the Bible. Within the institution of the Church itself learning and knowledge was no doubt somewhat broader, but still focused on a God-based curriculum. There was no incentive to look beyond such curriculum for knowledge. Under such a static outlook there was little change, or desire for change, in a status quo.

Over the past six or seven hundred years, beginning about the 13th century, man, at least Western man, has increasingly demonstrated a curiosity regarding his surroundings. That led him to question the status quo of his time. Today we, you and I, are largely the beneficiaries of this curiosity and its resultant benefits, materialistically speaking. But, you may ask, is that all there is to it, the materialistic? The answer here has to be yes . . . and no. It seems that man is at once an optimist and a pessimist regarding himself and the world he inhabits.

It's not, and never has been, a naturally "kind and gentle" world for most of us although we do seem to be moving towards a kinder and more gentle world as time—lots of time—goes by. That's the optimistic view. The more pessimistic view is perhaps a shorter term consideration that we look at as we face our own mortal lifetimes, and man's sometimes inhumanity to man. Progress toward that kinder, gentler world isn't always apparent on this time frame. Therefore, to sustain and support ourselves we have developed a non-materialistic approach of looking at things. We generally refer to this as religion, the alternative to materialism.

Religion, broadly speaking, is a set of beliefs concerning the cause, nature and purpose of the universe. It is usually presented as the creation of a divinity, or superhuman agency (a god), and usually involving devotional and ritual observances. It often has a moral code for the conduct of human affairs. This non-materialistic approach to what is, why it is and what caused it is supportive of man's personal needs when and if the materialistic seems to offer or provide little or no encouragement or answers to life's difficult questions. It fulfills an apparent spiritual (psychic) need as well as the more visible materialistic needs of humanity. Some religions also address the issue of man's mortality.

Over time, it has come to be common and normal, at least in the West, for most to recognize both a materialistic and spiritual demand in life in some proportion. One purpose here as we move through these pages is to ask just what that proportion should be, perhaps even should it be. That is, does Western religion—today— fill a meaningful and even necessary role in the lives of humanity as we struggle to continue to move toward that more kinder, gentler world most would favor?

I would propose that generally it does. But I do so with the caveat that it would behoove it to reevaluate its purpose or role today as well as its credulity under current day conditions and future expectations. This might possibly affect its teachings. Actually, I see signs that this is underway in at least some quarters. The question is, as with some of the more progressive recommendations of the mid-twentieth century's Roman Catholic convocation of bishops known as Vatican II (1962-1965) for example, will proposed change be embraced, or strongly resisted by the beneficiaries of the status quo?

A case in point here might be the promulgation following Vatican II of *Nostara Aetate*, one of the shortest but conceivably among the most influential of the major documents to come out of this conclave. It is by many considered a watershed in the field of Christian-Jewish relations, not merely for what it said, but because of the radically new direction it encouraged. Some fifty years on now, it is still a work in process. It's not easy to modify religious policies, beliefs and teachings held for centuries. But this example shows it may be possible. Let's hope so.

Chapter Two

Looking Back to Look Ahead

Human history is replete with stories of "spirits" and "gods." Earliest man accepted spirits, both good and evil, for the worldly happenings he could not understand or explain. Myths were passed down by word of mouth. Rituals were developed to try to appease, or please such spirits and gods. A class of individual, the shaman, or witchdoctor or soothsayer and subsequently the priest developed to act specifically as an intermediary between people and gods. In all this, the spirits and gods were not necessarily thought of as supernatural but part of nature, initially. Often, sacrifices were called for to appease these spirits and gods, either to gain favor or to avoid disaster. This became a natural way of life in antiquity. Few probably questioned it. Gods served a human need for causality.

In pre-Christian (and in Christian) times both the Greeks and Romans had pantheons (temples) of gods. Often, these gods could take on human form. They acted and behaved in many ways like humans did; had faults and favorites. They lived in these temples, or on top of mountains. They were believable because they acted in many ways as humans but with superhuman powers to account for the physical events still a mystery to ordinary man. That was their primary difference. These gods were often transplants. If someone else's god appeared better or more powerful than a local god, it might be adopted, or at least some of its attributes bestowed upon the local deities. Significantly, these gods were at times said to interact with normal people.

In time, these spirits and gods were said to be active in history. That is, they walked with and spoke with humans. The Hebrew Bible is full of such interactions in the books of Genesis and Exodus. They are harder to find thereafter. In the New Testament, the closest such direct interaction in history is the saying attributed at the baptism of Jesus: "This is my Son, whom I love; with him I am well pleased." [1] It's not clear from the New Testament's three Synoptic Gospels, just who heard these words.

The biblical book of Exodus goes back at least 3,200 years; Genesis even further back, perhaps 4,500 years. These were not codified back then but rather the events that are depicted in these books date from these times. The books themselves are considered to be the recording of stories passed down by word of mouth over hundreds and hundreds of years, and from within the entire Middle East (Mesopotamia), and by multiple authors. Historical evidence today finds duplicates, if not exact duplicates very similar ones, in the histories and stories of different peoples at different times (the Flood and Creation narratives, for example).

With the Hebrew Bible we get a story of the development and subsequent history of a tribal people, the Jews, and the particular part that a god (or gods) plays in their history. From the story of Abraham (Genesis 17 for example), it would appear that this particular god—who referred to itself as "God Almighty"—was out evangelizing and as an enticement to him made a covenant with Abraham that if he would keep God Almighty's commandment (circumcision, at this point) and worship It, this god would make him a father of many nations; very fruitful. This god would make nations of him and kings would come from him. The covenant would be everlasting between this god and Abraham and his descendants for the generations to come. The whole land of Canaan, where Abraham was then an alien resident, this god would give as an everlasting possession to him and his descendants, and this god would be "their god." Now that's quite a promise, but with stipulations: follow me, obey me. That sounds suspiciously like what today we might call a Godfather's offer you can't refuse. One could speculate that this God Almighty must have been pretty hard up for followers to offer so much.

This was the beginning of a rocky history for the Jews. This god's promises were not immediately forthcoming, and it appears that not all of the descendants supported and followed this God Almighty all the time. At any rate, we jump forward in time and history to about the year 1,246 BCE to the prophet Moses and the exodus from Egypt. Biblically it appears that the God of Abraham (?) at this point is leading them out of captivity in Egypt by his agent, Moses, and towards the promised land of Canaan. Again, the journey is not direct, and the Jews seem less than united in their acceptance, commitment to or maintenance of covenantal requirements of this God Almighty.

During this exodus Moses, the acknowledged leader of and judge for most of these people, spends an inordinate amount of time resolving disputes between individuals brought to him by the Israelites (or Jews): "They stood around him from morning till evening. His-father-in-law Jethro said, 'what is this you are doing for the people? Why do you alone sit as judge, while all these people stand around you from morning till evening?' Moses answered him, 'because the people come to me to seek God's will. Whenever they have a dispute, it is brought to me, and I decide between the parties and inform them of God's decrees and laws.'" [2] It would seem Moses was privy to these divine guidelines even before he spent those forty days on the mountain formally receiving them.

The point here is that in this moving mass of people disputes arose, as would be normal, and there were no—what we would call civil or criminal—laws or established set of rules or regulations to fall back on other than the "Will of God." And most did not know the Will of God, and so sought those who were supposed to be in such possession to settle matters in an authoritative and acceptable manner. To quote a seemingly truism, necessity is the mother of invention. What was needed at this time and place was a documented system of laws and decrees that reflected the Will of God. A documented system knowable and available to all and not just through a few or only one judge thought to be familiar with these matters. Through necessity, and by the work of mortals, a set, a very detailed set, of "God's laws and decrees" was developed and enforced by a legion of judges appointed by a mortal, Moses.[3]

The idea of God, the presence of the god of the idea and most importantly the authority of that god was involved and invoked in the development and promulgation of these detailed rules for living. But no one save Moses, and perhaps a few elders of the tribe, were involved directly with God in so doing. If these rules and regulations were the Will of God, they were the result of mortal man needing, requesting and bringing them forth. And remember, all this was accomplished in a "closed door" meeting, so to speak. It was Moses and company that went up the mountain and forty days later came down the mountain with "the law." The purpose was purely this-worldly for the social stability and harmony of people in a community. But the necessary authority for these laws and decrees was "above man." These were delivered as divine commandments that needed to be followed under threat of divine retribution. Whether they were, or not, the people believed—and that was key—that they were.

That was an authority beyond question. The people, comparatively speaking, thereafter have a pretty complete set of laws and decrees by which to regulate the life of the community and the individual. From this "divine" legislative beginning, they are expanded significantly to involve all matters of life for the Jews under the direction of a mortal theocracy. It was, to say the least, convenient to have some authority "above man" to provide these decrees; no appeal was possible.

The point of this example is to demonstrate exactly what I meant when I said at the beginning, I believe in the concept of God. More exactly, it is in the utility—the usefulness—of the supreme concept of the good—of God—I believe in; the cultural, social and moral value imperative of the idea of God in arranging man's earthly affairs. Just how much authority do you think these "Ten Commandments" would have had if Moses and company had just presented them as their own thoughts as to how their group should act and behave? The idea of God, the promotion of religion supporting and guiding this idea, seems a logical and rational normal outgrowth of the concept itself, originally conceived as a convenience to explain the unexplainable to mortal man through the ages.

God Almighty—or at least God—becomes the ever-present authority for the Jewish people. The ultimate judge of human behavior; the source of hope and inspiration for the human condition and eventually the ultimate provider of life everlasting for those who, in God's view, deserve it. That's a powerful metaphor for a father (or mother) figure to the immature needing guidance, support and protection. And from today's perspective, mankind in that era could certainly be referred to as culturally, economically, and no doubt morally immature, whiggish as that judgment might appear. The concept of God in the life of mortal man is easily understood by man, and the utility of the concept seems evident. As we will see further in Chapter Five, the idea of God provides for three clear and very basic yearnings of mankind.

God under these assumptions (explaining the unexplainable) is a manifestation of the mind—a coming into being readily perceived by the understanding—eventually a mythology, or legend, for the benefit of man. Myths over the millenniums have been supportive of mankind and its societies in their attempts to reconcile the known with the unknown; the material (the seen) with the spiritual (the unseen). Jesus of Nazareth, the Christian Christ, was in all probability a historical figure. We have evidence for this apart from the Bible. But in keeping with the utility of the idea of God, much of what we are told about him, the Church's Christology, is no doubt legendary, mythological—for our benefit. He served a purpose. Many today continue to believe this. Jesus, as presented, represents our Christian path, or "bridge," to salvation. Who among us is not in favor of his or her own salvation? If the God Almighty of antiquity seems no longer available in history, or even so desirable any longer, Jesus (as a successor representative of this utilitarian idea of a deity for Christians) has served as an effective Church-promoted substitute, or proxy.

Why does the mental and projected image of this idea of God, this God Almighty, look so much like mortal man, at least in the West? Is it simply coincidence that the Christian (or Hebrew) God seems so anthropomorphic, so human-like, in our understanding? Of course not, we may argue. After all, we were purportedly created in his image. But just how? Physically, morally, spiritually, or just how? Looking in the mirror probably isn't a good suggestion. If we are created in his image, do we possess (at least in theory) his omnipotence, or omniscience (I exclude his omnipresence, even in this day and age of instant communication and worldwide travel. I simply can't see how we could be everyplace at once—my definition of chaos).

If we were created in God's image, how could we be bad? How could the "fall" ever have taken place? I know, yes, "evil" entered the world. From where? How? Well, from heaven; by fallen angels. If that is truly the explanation, then heaven seems no more (well, maybe a little more) perfect than our world.

This is simply not a rationally sound explanation for a world purportedly created in six of our time days by the Hebrew/Christian God, or by God's Wisdom or Word/Logos, and declared good by its own examination. Both the world and everything created in and for it is good, or it isn't. If it isn't then this God Almighty isn't what it has been built up to be. By whom? By mortal man.

If the biblical God Almighty is as claimed omnipotent, omniscience and the Creator of all, it seems impossible for it to have created such a scenario as unfolds in the Bible, or has pretty much existed in history ever since. Looking to such a God Almighty for salvation, individually or collectively, seems betting on the wrong horse, in what for us appears to be a one-horse race. The Church finds utility and security, if not comfort, in exploiting this concept of God over time. If things go well, God is being faithful and blessing us; if not, we must be bad and God—directly or through God's agent(s)—is, justifiably, punishing us. That's a win-win situation, for the Church.

As mortal time (history) has moved on, we see less of God in it, and more of the institution of the Church, presumably as God's agent;

the Bride of Christ. But that's the history of an institution founded upon a 2,000 to 4,500-year-old story of questionable antecedents. A story clinging to ancient beliefs in an attempt to protect and promote, if not itself, the very foundation of its being, which amounts to the same thing. Such beliefs are now long questioned, challenged in the face of what I describe as progress. Humankind has progressed. The Church, since at least the fifth or sixth century, even considering the Reformation, theologically has not—cannot and still be faithful to those historical core beliefs. That's a problem for the Church, and for the rest of us as well.

What is the natural response when your back is to the wall? You fight harder, or give up. The Church seems to be doing neither. It is just keeping on keeping on, so to speak. Mainstream religion may attempt to package and market its story in an updated presentation, but a rose by any other name remains a rose. And the result? A slow steady loss of followers. I believe, and polls seem to bear this out, most people lose their faith in religion before they lose their faith in God. Why? Because, like me, they continue to believe, consciously or unconsciously, in the idea of God.

So, if the God Almighty of the Bible presentation is in reality a myth, then at least the first chapter of it must also be mythological. That seems a plausible argument. A recent biography of the *Book of Genesis* by Ronald Hendel (Lives of Great Religious Books series) explains that Genesis "envisions a single, God-created universe in which human life is limited by the boundaries of knowledge and death. There is often a harsh realism in the Genesis accounts of human life."[4] That would certainly make sense, especially if it were man writing of what man knew of life, in his own lifetime. The fact that these were attributed to a god (man's scapegoat?) makes even more sense.

And as a further thought here, a bit more about salvation. Not individual salvation, but for you and me as members of mankind around the world. My perspective of God working any plan for overall salvation—life everlasting (and I know of nothing biblically about the collective, unless you define God's plan for individuals in the collective sense)—isn't pretty, as far as I can see.

What kind of a benevolent, merciful and supposedly just Creator starts off the history of his creation of humanity by kicking out of their home his two morally innocent (in my view) figures which he created for one act—just one—of disobedience; by indiscriminately wiping out his entire human creation (save one family) in a flood for their unacceptable behavior; at Babel disrupting their mortal abilities to easily communicate with each other, creating separation and suspicion in the minds of his creation? That sounds more like vengeance, not salvation, at least as I understand it. If you happen to be a Premillennialist Christian anticipating God to carry away the elect, i.e., "the rapture," the Book of Revelations is right up your alley. If not, it's hard to see it in this day and age as inspired by a loving and just God (especially if you happen to be Jewish!).

Next, after promising one single individual (Abraham) great things for his descendants, God Almighty (El, the Canaanite High God, it would appear) seems to leave the scene for almost 650 of our years while those descendants of Abraham struggle to make it. We pick up the story again in Egypt where the descendants of Abraham, now the Jews, are having a difficult time (according to their own story). They were, after all, migrants into Egypt. Now after some 400 years of servitude there, a current god (Yahweh, it would appear out of Midian, as opposed to El out of Canaan) apparently promotes a savior for the Jews, Moses. Under his leadership they escape Egypt and after a number of years of wandering in the desert (not really all desert, but more like the steppes of Russia. They were, after all, mostly tribal groups of roving stock shepherds) arrive at the "promised land." Thus Yahweh settles on adopting this tribal group, the Jews, to use as means to his ends. This, at least early on per the Bible, is not all that successful either for Yahweh or the Jews. But hey, it's a start.

Chapter Three

The Church's Story

When does doubt start to creep in?

For centuries, proponents in each of the three god-religions—Judaism, Christianity and later Islam—had understood that God was not merely another being. It did not exist like the other phenomena we experience. In Eastern thought the Absolute, which is the inner essence of all things, is a void, a nothing. It has no existence in the normal sense. In the West, however, Christians got more and more into the habit of talking about God as though it really *were* one of the things that existed. Recall that early on Jesus is purported to have referred to "God the Father," and "our Father who art in Heaven." Later, the West seized upon the new science in an attempt to prove the objective reality of God as though he could be tested and analyzed like anything else.[1] Western theology had tended to overemphasize the importance of rationality ever since Thomas Aquinas, a tendency which had increased since the Reformation.[2] To date, however, science has not been the handmaiden of religion.

During the nineteenth century, one major philosopher after another rose to challenge the traditional view of God, at least the "God" who prevailed in the West. They were particularly offended by the notion of a supernatural deity "out there" which had an objective existence. That idea of God as the Supreme Being had gained ascendance in the West. Other monotheistic traditions had gone out of their way to separate themselves from this type of theology.

Over the centuries, the West had gradually lost sight of this more imaginative conception of God. Catholics and Protestants had come to regard "him" as a Being who was another reality added on to the world we know, overseeing our activities like a celestial Big Brother, or Heavenly Father. Not unsurprisingly, this notion of God was quite unacceptable to many people in the post-revolutionary world, since it seemed to condemn human beings to an ignoble servitude and an unworthy dependence that was incompatible with human dignity.[3]

And here we are, in the West, two thousand years on and counting; still awaiting the arrival of the Christian Church's promised second coming of Jesus (the Parousia) and subsequent establishment of the kingdom of God. What are we to make of what we are taught of and about the Christian Triune God? Do you believe in it? I try, but in all honesty, I have doubts, as have many others throughout history. Even within Christianity, Eastern and Western Churches seem to have different understandings of it, as we'll see. As I said, Trinity or no Trinity, I do strongly believe in the idea of God, but I'm unsure that such belief makes God itself a reality. But, maybe.

Does that really matter to anyone but myself or in your case, to you? After all, religious belief is a private personal matter. At least in our country no one can tell you how to believe, or even to believe. But yes, I think so. I think it matters more broadly than just you or me because of the ongoing historical and contemporary impact of the Christian religion's questionable (I claim) gospel message (they claim) regarding belief and its cultural, social and political impact: believe the "good news," or be eternally damned. To me that's more of a clear threat as opposed to an invitation. Although I do admit you hear this less and less often, it seems, in many churches today than in times past. Do you ever wonder why this is?

We know of the Christian God through the teaching of the Catholic (universal) Church, in all its many manifestations. The Church, in its turn, relies upon the revealed (or at least inspired) Hebrew/Christian Bible for its source of testimony concerning God. How are we to know if the Church is correct in its affirmation of God? Because, says the Church, the Bible tells us so. Some append to this source of circular proof (that scripture is interpreted by scripture) an exhortation to, "Look around you. See just what the Lord (God) has done," as the Bible claims, and is doing through (His) people."

Okay, but just how does the Church know that the Bible is true and correct, or that what we look around at is truly the work of such a God? Because, in the case of the Bible, it *believes* it is. And, in some aspects, the biblical presentation is historically verifiable in time, place and detail as histories should be. Does that, in itself, make its word, its message, literally true? Not necessarily, but it does make it more credible. And that's the critical value of the Bible to the Church: it believes it to be true—it has no other basis—and conceives of its mission to convince as many people as possible of its truth, as it interprets it. Why? Because the Christian Bible supposedly exhorts it to. As to whether or not this was Jesus' exhortation, or the Church's is a historically debatable issue for scholars (Some evidence stemming from historical criticism seems to favor it being the Church's self-promotional exhortation).

So, if that's how the Church knows God, through belief of and faith in the revealed word of the Bible, how does it convince me (should I need "convincing?") to believe? Just like the Church believes, through study and instruction leading to faith and trust in the Bible. It is made easier for us because the Church is professional; it purports to be an expert on the Bible and has centuries of experience in biblical exegesis and study that it can use to dogmatically explain, in the Western sense of the term, questions we might have about God and the revealed word of the Bible. This faith in and dogmatic understanding of matters surrounding God also gives the Church a degree of "moral suasion" to do the right thing which is, in their eyes, believe in God as the Church presents God. To the Church, and to those individuals who believe, it amounts to a self-evident necessity. (Again, should you and I need convincing of a purported self-evident necessity?)

But belief is not a one-way street. The Church's efforts here have historically been made easier by the felt need of the individual to have some acceptable explanation for worldly matters and events beyond their experience and understanding as well as some meaning—even compensation—for often dismal worldly circumstances. It has historically offered biblical (and at times extra-biblical) rationale for how and why things are as they are, and "hope" in an improved next life for those who have little reason to expect better days in their present worldly life circumstances. But this "carrot" has also been used historically as a stick with which to threaten individuals who do not believe according to the Church that they may receive no reward in the purported afterlife. On the contrary, they may be subject to eternal "damnation."[4] That, I would think in times past, would be a great incentive for most anyone to "believe" or at least try and want to believe. You and I might question this in a post-enlightenment (freethinking) world.

But what about you and me personally? Do we believe? I've already suggested my skepticism—really my disbelief at this point. We live in a largely Christian culture and been exposed to the (Protestant/Catholic/Orthodox) Christian faith most of our lives. I don't know about you, but I have been a regular church-goer for many years. Do I believe in this revealed God? Am I a member of their faith as opposed to simply a member of their congregation? Probably not really, in a way they expect. Then can I sincerely believe in what they preach? Obviously not, at this point in what the Church describes as my "faith journey." I find the Church's arguments often persuasive, but far from compelling. You may or may not feel the same.

I find merit in the work of the Church in the here and now community. There is of course a clear biblical basis for this. But increasingly, it seems to me, this is the result of the Church's felt need to justify itself today in a socially, economically and culturally progressive world working with an eons old script; a Church whose vision of spreading the original message of Jesus—"Repent, for the kingdom of God is near"[5]—seems far less pressing, at least here in America; one which long ago morphed for most from an apocalyptic mindset to one of philosophic platonic expectations. This seems, aside from the most hidebound fundamentalist approach to belief, a Church increasingly focused on worldly as opposed to otherworldly matters and concerns—always in the name of God's earthly proxy, Jesus.

Sin and my soul seem less a concern than my worldly condition and comfort as is attending to those conditions of other congregants and rectifying the conditions of the underprivileged in the community—and the world. That in itself does not seem a bad mission; just an evolving (justifying) one from the original Christian message of preparing for the imminent return of Christ and final judgment and salvation (or not). It should none the less probably be recognized that some Christian denominations continue to be focused more on the original message than most.

This issue, at least here I refer to it as an issue, of the Church's apparent shifting of focus or emphasis from God to the community—all in the name of God, of course—apparently is recognized by others as well. One gentleman writing a letter to the editor in *The Christian Century* magazine put it this way [paraphrasing]:

"Of course the Church needs to be engaged in the world. But Christians are not 'accidental conspirators'; we are a people called by God to witness to his grace and mercy. We get the power and tools to do that through encountering the triune God. This vision of renewal seems more like reinvention of the Church. Like so many others today, the article assumes that the purpose of God and our calling is to make the world a better place so we can all be happy and healthy and live peacefully. Such teaching makes God unnecessary, and the Church simply a gathering of like-minded individuals."[6]

His major point seems to be that if all you are interested in is doing good works within the community, become a Lion or a Rotarian. His point regarding the purpose of God is one we will focus on in Chapters Five and Six.

So, to get at the question raised above, do you believe, really believe, in the three persons of the Triune God of the Christian Bible? It seems that to "come to God" you must know or be aware of, and can—actually need to—believe in God on two levels: an emotional level and an intellectual level. One might refer to these as a want or desire to believe and a fact-based probability, a conviction enabling belief (colloquially sometimes referred to as the "heat" and "light" of religion). What happens when these two faith sources fail to support each other? It produces, in my case, doubt. The Self asserts, "Yes, I do want to believe, but where is the truth here?" No matter what I may want, I ask myself, does God or doesn't God exist? Why can't I make up my mind? Only recently, have I clearly understood this bi-level issue. I wasn't aware of the cause of my unshakable skepticism on my almost life-long journey of faith, as it is called. One could say that the faster I ran here toward belief, the behinder I seemed to get as I studied more about theology, Christology and the history of the biblical God. Like one of those troubling dreams where it seems you can only move toward your objective in slow motion, never reaching it. Frustrating! How about you?

My (our) difficulty here may be symptomatic with how the Christian religion developed in the West. In Greek Orthodoxy, God remains entirely incomprehensible, "he stays within himself," in his eternal mystery. He is not another being, additional to the world. Some time ago now, the Eastern Church decided that an authentic theology must meet two criteria: it must be silent and paradoxical. In the West, however, theologians would continue to "talk and explain God." Some imagined that when they said God, the divine reality actually coincided with the ideas in their minds. Some would attribute their own thoughts and ideas to God, saying that God wanted this, forbid that, and had planned the other—in a way that seemed dangerously idolatrous.[7] Under such an active as opposed to passive theology, one—at least this one—naturally expects some substantiation to what is being preached. This, to me, has not been forthcoming.

Belief in God demands submission; the conviction (faith) of the truth of some doctrine or dogma which is the result of a voluntary act of will—the ability to desire an outcome. But my need and desire to believe stalls because it's not supported by my rational based ability to understand and accept. Faith is religion's answer to the challenge of reason. Again, St. Anselm (1033-1109) of Canterbury's maxim (based upon a saying of St. Augustine, or perhaps Boethius), "I believe so as to understand," shows great faith, which I plainly do not have. I simply cannot accept as trustworthy too many of the propositions underlying the Western Christian God argument (virgin birth, incarnation, transfiguration, transubstantiation, bodily resurrection, the efficacy of prayer, these most basic pillars of the faith, for example). By trustworthy I mean propositions supported by evidence sufficient to establish them as (at least highly probably) believable. Faith in God is just that: faith in God. I simply can't seem to firmly grasp it, though I strongly feel on the emotive level I should, and want to. Inquiry, study and contemplation both within and without the Church have been of little avail here.

The more I seem to learn about theology—in church as well as outside of church—the more difficult it is for my intellect to accept the orthodox Christian proposition. I'm advised you can neither prove nor disprove God rationally, and I am a rational being. You either believe, have faith and hope, or you don't. Right now, I don't. You might excuse my disbelief on the basis that, it is purported—at least by my church—it is only the Grace of God that allows belief. I have to date apparently not been so blessed with this gift.

Let's pause here for just a moment to look at this term "grace." Just what are we talking about here? Well, we're talking about the "Grace of God." Yes, but exactly what is it? The term gets thrown around pretty often in not just a few circumstances. It's put forth as an important theological point that we need to be clear on.

First of all, as understood today, grace appears to be primarily a New Testament (Christian) concept. The most oft quoted passage is probably Paul's in Romans chapter three: "This righteousness from God comes through faith in Jesus Christ to all who believe, and all are justified freely by his grace through the redemption that came by Christ Jesus."[8]

In the Old Testament, it (the Hebrew word *chesed)* can be used to designate kindness and graciousness, in general, with no particular tie or personal relationship between the individuals involved; and it's generally shown by a superior to an inferior when there is no obligation to do so. Coming from the New Testament it's (the Greek word *Charis)* been described by one Christian author as "...more than unmerited favor. It is reality. By grace you live, by grace you please God, grace is always based on who He is and what He has done. Grace is never based on who you are apart from Him or on what you can do."[9] Another religious group describes grace kinda along these lines: "When we speak of God's grace, we mean all the good gifts we enjoy freely in life. . . .This is the bedrock of grace—creation, life, human being."[10] These I would categorize as creative grace.

The other New Testament view of God's grace is of redemptive grace. This is focused most clearly on the life, death, and resurrection of Jesus, meaning the one chosen to deliver this particular grace. In the New Testament, grace indicates quite specifically God's redemptive love. It is always active to save the people and to keep them in relationship with God. St. Paul in the Book of Ephesians describes it this way: "For it is by grace you have been saved, and this is not from yourselves, it is the gift of God—not by works, so that no one can boast. For we are God's handiwork, created in Jesus Christ to do good works, which God prepared in advance for us to do."[11] Somewhat later the evangelist John put it this way: "For the Law was given through Moses; grace and truth came through Jesus Christ."[12]

So, we have what we might term creative grace, and redemptive grace, the latter being what probably comes to mind for most of us, most of the time. It is an unmerited gift of God without which, the Church implies, you and me and everyone else are hopeless. We are totally dependent upon the Grace of God—for apparently everything, both mortal and immortal. It cannot be earned. It's God's gift to give, if God sees fit to bestow it upon you. And, according to the Church, it is only available at their counter in exchange for your belief in and submission before Jesus, as defined and/or dictated by the Church. Some churches' offers seem more liberal than others.

In the case of the Catholic Church, you must deal with two forms of grace, sanctifying grace and actual grace. Sanctifying grace stays in the soul. Actual grace, by contrast, is transient. It doesn't live in the soul but acts on the soul from the outside. It gets the will and intellect moving so we can seek out and keep sanctifying grace. You need sanctifying grace to live in heaven. Oh my!

This gift of grace raises at once another one of those difficult to accept propositions I mention. If you can only believe by the Grace of God, then, assuming God, God must pick and choose who It grants the gift of belief. That seems somewhat exclusive but still consistent with the Church telling me God is inclusive in his salvation of "those who believe." Let's call this "Catch-23." Taking this to the next level of questionability brings predestination to the fore.

If God is all knowing, God has already determined who will be granted the gift of grace, and thus, who won't. If this is so, my desire or need to believe has little to no bearing on the issue. It's God's decision. This sounds to me like the Christian God is not one open to and for all. Rather the Christian God is for a certain chosen elect: those upon whom It has decided to extend its grace. So if as the Church preaches, we are all saved by grace alone through Jesus Christ, there are a lot of us who apparently stand little or no chance of salvation. If this is the case, then why make the effort? It's already a done deal. Still, there are two possible answers as to why; one active, the other passive.

The first was suggested by the seventeenth-century French Catholic philosopher Blaise Pascal. Pascal would "seek with groans," searching for truth and God while lamenting that he could find neither through reason. Pascal was convinced that (and preoccupied with) life's central question concerned death and immortality and that, in the face of certain annihilation, believing in God is a wager worth making. Many might agree with Pascal's thinking here. But to me, it sounds less of belief and more like taking out insurance. So if the theory of the gift of grace is correct, don't bother applying.

The second was suggested by the twentieth century theologian and philosopher Paul Tillich. During his theological studies at the University of Halle (1905-1912) he was forced to match the doctrinal position of the Lutheran Church, based on the established confessional documents, against the theological liberalism and scientific empiricism that dominated the academic scene (in Germany) at that time. His attention was directed to the doctrine of justification through faith, laid down by St. Paul and reiterated by

Martin Luther. Tillich concluded this doctrine, which he called the "Protestant principle," could be given a wider scope than previously had been thought. It could be understood to encompass not just how sinful man can be acceptable to a holy god, but man's intellectual life as well, and thus all of man's experiences. As the sinner is declared just in the sight of God, so the doubter is possessed of the truth even as he despairs of finding it.[13] One might put this thought alongside the concept of the Church visible and the Church invisible. The problem here I see is that Tillich's approach would appear to make divine grace an entitlement.

The main Christian proposition my intellect (rightly or wrongly) anguishes over is the Christology, the theological nature and character of Jesus of Nazareth, the Christ. In fact, it is more than just that. It's the very believability, or truth, of the claims Christianity makes about this indispensable prerequisite historical religious figure that I wrestle with. Here is a mustard seed in the granary of history. But in milling it the Church has transformed it into a finished flour both pungent and potent appearing. In presenting it (marketing it) to Western mankind the Church claims it represents an elixir for eternal life. But for those who find it unpalatable the Church threatens unpleasant consequences. Their message is both the carrot and the stick, all in one. The claims the Church makes for Christianity (or itself), for what it offers and what it warns of, border on the incredible. Yet we are asked to believe, on faith alone, the incredible. That in itself seems staggering!

The itinerant first century charismatic Jewish holy man/healer/ prophet whose mentor was John the Baptist and who plied primarily the villages and backcountry of the small province of Galilee, Jesus of Nazareth, the Church tells us, was and *is* God, The God Almighty itself: God itself incarnate in one of the three of God's (Trinitarian) Christian manifestations—"*The Word became flesh.*" Now this biblical claim by the evangelist who penned the biblical Gospel of John in the late first or early second century, was only officially proclaimed orthodox some three hundred years after the fact. Just who recognized it? The Church bishops did, at least a majority of those few attending a convocation in Nicaea in May 325 did. It was not a unanimous declaration; it was man-made and questionably biblical. It did, in addition, make creation *ex nihilo* (from nothing) an official Christian doctrine for the first time. However, its critical ruling for the Church was insisting that The Creator (God) and Redeemer (Jesus) were one in substance (much more on this down the line here).

According to Christian scripture, Jesus was God incarnate (took on flesh), born of a virgin (disputable translation), was crucified and buried (taken down relatively soon after crucifixion and placed in a cave) and was bodily resurrected (came back to life) on the third day (by Jewish reckoning) following his crucifixion on the cross. That's the party line.

My current pastor, a learned churchman whom I respect for both his belief and breadth of biblical knowledge and understanding has told me, almost face-to-face you might say, that if I don't believe these four pillars of Christianity, then don't call myself/yourself a Christian. As shocking as this seemed at the time, he's right. If I cannot accept (believe) these scripturally purported "facts" about Jesus, I'm simply not a mainline—Presbyterian in this case—traditional Christian. Ouch! As freethinking as I admit to being, I nevertheless considered myself one until that time some three or four years ago now. Since then, I have pondered this issue with greater angst. This goes back to the two faith sources, need/desire and conviction. I simply can't get them to move forward together, try as I might. I remain increasingly deeply skeptical. What about you?

But there's even more entangling issues the Church can't quite seem to get free of, or reconcile with today's liberal culture.

Chapter Four

The Church's Story II

Here's a tough one: assume you (The Church—reformed or not) profess to have the unchanging truth, about everything, revealed through a sacred book going back over three thousand years. Assume further that you spend centuries promoting and defending this truth and its source. You demand that people recognize it and live by its commandments which you are exclusively empowered to interpret, teach and enforce; and to the wayward you proclaim unbelief faces both mortal and immortal consequences. Question: How easy is credibly varying from this authoritative claim?

It's certainly not going to be something easy to navigate. Not only is varying from the historical script the issue, more basic perhaps is accepting that the script is or may be flawed—or incorrectly interpreted—in some very obvious way. How can it be? It already possesses the truth, what the Bible says or implies about this. Remember, scripture interprets scripture, and truth cannot contradict truth. For the Church to accept even the idea of change could be to admit error. How many of us like to do that?

But the history of mankind is generally and for the most part a story of progress, of change, certainly after the Dark Ages from the fall of Rome in 493 through about the tenth century. Not smoothly or even consistently but over time accumulated knowledge of the universe, our little world, and ourselves has been cause for reevaluating things we thought we knew and understood. This, in fits and starts, has been going on pretty steadily since about the eleventh century now. It really took off in what we describe as the Renaissance of the fifteenth and sixteenth centuries and the French and English Enlightenments of the seventeenth and eighteenth centuries. Since that time, knowledge and worldly understanding have expanded without historical precedent, both for the individual in Western societies, and for mankind corporately, almost every place on earth.

Does that mean you and I (mankind) are smart? Yes it does, at least on a relative scale. And does that imply that the Church, as an institution, is not smart, or is stupid? Absolutely not. It means only that officially the Church is static in its view of reality. Its original focus was on less worldly concerns. It was focused on "saving" you and me—"Repent, for the kingdom of God is at hand!" The Church in times past claimed to speak for all aspects of life in preparation for the kingdom, and/or for the afterlife. It has in the face of both the extended delay in any second coming of Christ (the Parousia) and the apparent earthly progress of humanity increasingly been forced into the position of trying to accommodate change, without itself changing. It often claims today that the proper spheres of responsibilities for the Church differ from the spheres of responsibility for a more material and increasingly scientific understanding and application of "truth." There is the rule of God's law (vertical truth, according to Catholicism) and the rule of man's law (horizontal truth, again, per the Pope), and when the two come in to conflict, the Church often finds itself in a difficult modern day position concerning God's law (more on this in Chapter Nine).

Modern man may well be in the wrong over the longer term, but the Church over the long term has been less than totally successful in stemming the tide of "progress" in the worldly affairs of man. And there are good reasons for this. Consider the message of the biblical Book of Ecclesiastes a good example:

"As the author (unknown, but some suspect King Solomon) looks about at the human enterprise, he sees man in mad pursuit of one thing and then another—laboring as if he could master the world, lay bare its secrets, change its fundamental structure, break through the bounds of human limitations and master his own destiny—he sees man vainly pursuing hope and expectations that in reality are 'meaningless, a chasing after the wind.' But faith teaches him that God has ordered all things according to its own purposes, and that man's role is to accept these, including his own limitations as God's appointments. Man, therefore, should be patient and enjoy life as God gives it. He should know his own limitations and not vex himself with unrealistic expectations…"[1]

Man according to this work is powerless; progress in the human condition, understanding or control over his own destiny is an illusion. Nonetheless, man has indeed done much of what this book rejects as meaningless, a chasing after the wind. Today we can know the path of that wind, and how a baby is formed within the mother and so much more that in the days of this book was simply not conceivable. Rightly or wrongly, we call this progress, and it stands in often stark contrast to claims in this Judeo-Christian Book of Books.

What you and I know for a fact, or at least with a very high degree of probability, conflicts with or contradicts the sacred text in many ways: the earth is basically round; we understand why the sun will appear—we still say "come up"—in the East in the morning; we can know even the sex of unborn babies as well as the source of the wind or the causes of diseases. The stars will not fall to earth and the earth is not the center of the universe. Much of what we know today appears to contradict the Bible, directly and/or indirectly and/or the teachings of the Church.

This present day political and social liberalization, expanding knowledge base and education makes it difficult for some of us to believe in the God of the Bible; to have faith in the Church. We may sincerely want to but perceive that the teaching of one, based on revelation, is too often at odds with the teaching of the other, based on reason. Faith and belief, as I pointed out above, need a commitment on two levels: the emotive and the intellectual. If you accept the biblical creation of man, how can you accept the theory of evolution (although some do try to)? If you understand the universe in terms of today's science, where is (physically) the heaven where the kingdom of God already exists, and where the Church assures us we are eventually to (physically) enter? These are not intended to be trick questions for the Church.

If the phrase the kingdom of God, or heaven on earth, is simply a metaphor for a new Eden or for an improved social, economic, and political world—which you might argue we are slowly achieving—why has it taken this biblical God so long to achieve it; to bring about our salvation? Yes, I know, the Church has answers, especially to this last question. But they are answers from well-meaning but self-interested procrastinators relying on a script over three thousand years old. How believable, considering context, can this be in today's world for what appears to be an increasing number of people? That's my argument; that is what produces doubt. Always the same old story. For a deity supposedly omnipotent, omniscient, and omnipresent, the Bible's God seems to me, and maybe to you, rather inept according to today's standards, and to be conspicuously absent from today's world. We seem to be pretty much on our own here in how things are being run and what is happening to mankind generally as we stagger towards the future. The Church, no doubt, would question this latter claim.

Enter into our world the Prince of Darkness. Its objective is to thwart God and lead man astray. Just where did it come from if God created everything—and it was good? "Bad" angels... hummm. Yes, admittedly there is conflict; yes there is bad in our world of yesterday and today (which, again, God biblically declared good prior to biblically wiping out mankind in a flood and starting over again—fool me once (in the Garden of Eden), shame on you; fool me twice (in the flood), shame on me! But, the Church tells us, this too will pass. In the end, God will overcome the Prince of Darkness's assault of conflict and the bad in our world. Then God will reign supreme. Okay, maybe; I hope so. But what good does that do each succeeding generation of believers who have had to, and continue to have to, endure the present? They will be rewarded in the Hereafter, assures the Church. But what beyond "hope" and faith through belief in their God of the Bible does the Church provide here, which seems significantly less than a bird-in-hand?

Furthermore, if this Greek platonic Hereafter Christianity has adopted and promotes is so attractive and true, why need mankind spend so much time living what for too many is a cruel or even punishing life here on earth? Or, for those enjoying a modestly comfortable life here on earth, why should they face the specter of God's rejection? Recall that the first (those enjoying a modestly comfortable life on earth) will be last in the Kingdom of God, according to the Bible.[2] And their guilt? Only of being neither of the poor, nor presumably the weak or the humble who are biblically given priority to inherit the earth in the kingdom of heaven. Why should they get all the good seats? Agreed they may well have had it pretty rough here as mortals, but can't people who are at least modestly successful be considered good and worthy Christians too? Well, responds the Church, we don't know: "it's a mystery" (there it is again!). But don't lose faith. God has a plan for us.

Ah, a plan. And that is supposed to satisfy, to comfort you and me? God has a plan? Absolutely, says the Church. God has a plan for our salvation, whether or not we recognize it. Okay, let's look at this. This raises the question, just what constitutes a plan; and what exactly do you (Church) mean by our salvation?

First salvation: it means, according to St. Paul, eternal life through belief in Jesus Christ.[3] But note that a belief in an afterlife was developing some time before the appearance of the man from Nazareth. It most likely arrived in Palestine via ancient Egypt, maybe Persia (present day Iran). The ancient Egyptians were the first people who developed fully worked out beliefs about personal immortality and who connected an afterlife with good and evil conduct in this world. What began as an afterlife available only to the ruling pharaohs quickly democratized into a widespread belief in the possibility of resurrection for everyone.[4] The notion of life ever-after is not a Christian creation.

Still, biblically, the plan that God had/has for mankind appears to be in Jesus, according to the Church. God uses Jesus (in a Western understanding, one of its three itself's) to save mankind from their selves. Just how this supposedly works is spelled out below in the discussion of atonement. The fulfillment for us is in the Christ who is the resurrection and the life. According to the Gospel of John Jesus said, "I am the resurrection and the life. He who believes in me will live, *even though he dies;* and whoever lives and believes in me will never die."[5]

Well, okay. If that was/is the plan—belief in the Church's evolved version of Jesus—I would offer that the Gospel of John, authored by one who in the scope of things was rather a latter-day Greek philosophically leaning evangelist (gospel writer), needs updating; he needs to round that out a bit as he sits there in the early Church's pulpit.

Today, it seems demonstrably questionable at least at the rational—let alone the biological—level: "He who believes in me will live, *even though he dies.*" Has the Church today nothing more "enlightened" to offer than this two-thousand-year-old bromide delivered in a gospel considered a late-comer and very much in the Church's corner according to at least some knowledgeable biblical historians (my reading of E.P. Sanders, and Geza Vermes, for example)?

If it hasn't, if this is all it can come up with, then perhaps that explains, at least in part, why the Church is losing its following. Between 1990 and 2013 the proportion of Americans who identify themselves as Christians declined from 86% to 71%, an almost 16% drop. Should this trend continue, in less than three decades, we could well see less than 50% of Americans identifying themselves as Christians. So what? I'm not sure, but it certainly could reflect a rejection of the Church's teaching, or at minimum the presentation of its message. But the Church throughout history, and continuing today, has been a force in human affairs. Who or what will replace it, if anything, in the future we are presumably facing? Let me comment on that below. For now, let me just note that it also means there will be a lot more real estate on the market.

In America, there is less than half the number of churches today than there were only 100 years ago. Since 1950 there are one-third fewer churches in America.[6] In Germany, 515 Catholic churches closed over the past decade. The Roman Catholic leaders in Holland estimate that within a decade two-thirds of their 1,600 churches will be closed and 700 of the country's Protestant churches will likely close over the next four years.[7]

Bottom line, it's hard, very hard, to sustain and defend an unchangeable story in an evolving, almost contradictory world. This is what the Church has been attempting to do. It has to. If it holds the truth in its particularism as it proclaims, then the rest of humanity must (has to) be wrong. The situation seems to be that fewer and fewer believe, or at least believe that the Church has a meaningful (credible) "truth" story in today's progressive, increasingly knowledgeable liberal world. The evidence simple fails pragmatically to support it (orthodox theology, i.e., that within the main consensus, scripture and the Church are always equally true. However, given context, it may not always be relevant). As one liberal theologian has put it—as sarcastic as it sounds—the Church appears to be asking you to deposit your brain at the door as you enter for worship. You may pick it up on your way out.[8]

Still, you may believe; you may have faith in it. Hope, which represents comfort in the present, aside from any social agenda, seems all the Church has to offer. That, it should be pointed out, is not insignificant and for some that may be enough. I don't know about you, but for me it falls short. Loaded down with my skepticism, I have not (yet) been granted that necessary Grace of God enabling belief; probably never will be. So my journey of faith doesn't look like it's going anyplace other than right where I'm at. At my age, where I'm at is about as far ahead as I dare look.

But I should in all fairness to the Church point out what seems to be a truism, at least in the realm of philosophy. Maybe it applies to theology: philosophy, at its best, probably doesn't have to progress that much, because the most difficult and most important human problems don't change that much. To the degree that theology deals with important human problems, maybe it doesn't have to change that much either. Maybe the Church simply has to recognize, even if this

means updating the script, what those religiously important human problems are. Then it would need to address them in a manner that is reflective of this intent, possibly reorienting its basic message about our salvation. Easy to suggest. But a hellofalot harder to accomplish, I realize. Specifically, what about Jesus?

He purportedly came, according to the Church, to save mankind. Or in his historical perspective and own understanding, specifically the Jews. The idea of God was around a long time before Jesus of Nazareth came on the scene. And his promotion (by learned *men*) to co-equal, meaning here "of the same substance" as God— or *Homoousia,* in the Greek—was by no means immediate nor recognized even by those he worked among. In fact, it was several centuries before the Church Fathers got around to so declaring, and just how, at the Church Councils of Nicaea (325) and Chalcedon (451).

Is it not possible that with the expanded knowledge and experience of the past sixteen hundred years, those councils could be "revisited," reinterpreted, or updated? Not to bow to progress, as such, but at least to acknowledge progress (or change), especially in human understanding of both ourselves and the material world on and in which we exist? This could result in a redefinition of the God/Jesus relationship, no easy feat! Nonetheless, at one time most of mankind believed, and taught, that the Sun revolved around the earth, and that the world was flat—that was the appearance to us. Today we and the Church know better. And today we seem, as a humanity, no worse off for it.

Maybe it's time we understood better about the why of God. Maybe there's another story, or at least another way of understanding the story we have of God. True, I'm assuming now that we can know. This I recognize is a contemporary Western Christian freethinking view, not a more orthodox one. This in spite of the fact that I above pointed out that one cannot know God rationally, or more correctly, one cannot prove God rationally. But maybe rational understanding is possible—understanding the basis of the god idea leading us to believe in the reality of God. This is a rational approach to understanding God that you (or at least I) seldom if ever hear put forth, although I know historically it's not an altogether new "thought-question" for many people. One such is professor of Hebrew Bible at the Collège de France Thomas Römer's recent book, *The Invention of God.* Another is the now retired liberal Episcopal bishop John Shelby Spong in his 1998 book *Why Christianity Must Change or Die.*

What if we brought reason and the lessons of time to bear and deduced that, for explanations rationally understandable, the Bible has what amounts to a chicken or the egg situation backwards: God didn't create man, as such; man over time and out of human necessity, really, created (perceived or became conscious of) the supernatural and ultimately the idea of the Judeo-Christian God. Hold on now: this may imply, but doesn't really mean, that God does not exist. It simply says that the mutual relationship and the manner in which man received the idea of God might well differ from the official (orthodox) Judeo-Christian historical presentation. [9]

Infamous blasphemy, shouts the Church and all sincere believers! I can't blame them. It's a rather radical proposal. But, let's examine it with as much calm, composure and evidence as we might be able to muster. Making this case may not be as difficult, nor as onerous, as it might first appear.

Chapter Five

Religious Reality: God vs. The Idea of God

Some sixteen hundred years ago St. Augustine, the bishop of Hippo said, "To think of God is to attempt to conceive something than which nothing more excellent or sublime exists, or could exist." But to think of God assumes that the notion, or the idea of God, is already present. What is the idea of God? What is the origin of the idea? Is it God? If so, how did we get it from God – is it innate or discovered in experience? Or, did we simply invent it?[1] Questions, questions, questions.

Historically the god-idea seems to have originated when civilization was still in its infancy. Primitive people, out of fear and admiration towards natural phenomena, had attributed such phenomena to spirits and "gods." In the beginning, peoples worshiped many gods—gods of trees, streams, lighting and thunder, storms, wind, the sun and all other terrestrial events. Almost anything beyond their comprehension was attributed to "spirits and gods." After all, something must be their cause or reason for.

Gradually, in the more civilized world (In Greek, the *oikumene*), from all these spirits/gods, there slowly over time grew a realization that the phenomena of the universe were not many but were one. In classical pagan cultures, it became widespread thinking that all of their various gods were really sub-gods, or different faces of one supreme deity. This understanding gave rise to the idea of the monotheistic god of recent ages. In the process of developing, the god-idea went through a variety of changing social and intellectual climates.

So, the idea of gods (later God) is probably one of the oldest, if not the oldest, widely-held impressions by man from pre-historic days to the present time. And over time, the idea expanded to what we see today. First it was the idea of a supernatural power that would, or at least could, if invoked, protect. Our earliest ancestors looked to "the gods" to protect them from the dangerous and uncontrollable, what we know today are natural (and largely predictable) physical occurrences, such as storms, earthquakes, floods, droughts and so forth.

At some point in time, no doubt with the aid of emerging religious (moral?) consciousness, the idea of God (now with a capital G) evolved and expanded to address the perceived imperfection of man. Man began to look at the idea of God not only for protection, but for the possibility of perfection; as an aspiration for betterment or improvement in the human condition in the mortal life he confronted. To be "God-like" was to be a better person, individually and collectively; something beyond man's individual grasp, absent such an ideal of perfection to aspire to.

And sometime even later (but well prior to St. Augustine's homily), Western religion encouraged the idea of God as an answer to our fear of human mortality. Civilized man was led to believe that the idea of God offered hope that believers in the idea might be granted, by the god of the idea, immortality; life in perpetuity. And so, in relatively recent times—say the last two thousand plus years, or so—this for most is what the idea of God represents: the three very basic human yearning for (1) Protection, (2) Perfection, and (3) Perpetuity.

Over time, dealing with the idea of God was regarded by different peoples in different ways. Some idealized the god of the idea as the King of heaven and earth; they had an impression of God as a person, a Being. Others thought of God as an abstract principle; some as a force, or a kind of spirit energy. Some raised the ideal of supreme deity to the highest heaven, while others brought it down to the lowest depths of the earth. Some pictured God in a paradise. Others made an idol and worshipped it. Some went so far as to say that there is no human salvation (perpetuity) without belief in God—no matter how much good you do, you will not receive the fruits of your actions unless you act out of a faith in God (a further religious refinement of the thinking of the Egyptians in this regard).

The theists said, "Yes" and went on to affirm that the god of the idea really did exist. The atheists said, "No" and went on to affirm that god did not really exist at all. The skeptics or agnostics said, "We do not nor cannot know." The Positivists said that the god-idea is a meaningless problem since the idea of the term "god" is not clear. Thus, there grew a variety of notions and beliefs and names for the god-idea: pantheism, idolatry, belief in a formless god, belief in many gods and goddesses, etc. The Hindu idea of divinity is quite different from the Christian God. The Christian idea of God is again different from other faiths. Thus, numerous religions came into existence; each one differed from the other and each one said that "God is One," and the divinity we worship is (of course) the correct One. But each employed the idea of God in arriving at their particular theological bias.

Both the god-idea and its associated creation myths have been protected and defended by the god-religions which need these myths to justify their existence and usefulness to human society. All the present-day god-religions—Judaism, Christianity, Islam—claim to have received their respective scriptures as Revelation; in other words, they all profess them to come directly from the one God. Each claims that their religion stands for Universal Peace and Universal Brotherhood and other such high ethical ideals.[2]

And so here we are, thousands of years on and the debate continues. The Theists say yes, God exists. The Atheists say, no, God does not exist; the Skeptics continue to throw up their hands in exasperation and the Positivists continue to hold it is a meaningless debate. Is that progress, or is that progress! Nonetheless, what some would call progress, albeit slow progress—in the form of the accumulated knowledge based upon the sciences—has expanded or at least changed the tone of this debate. Where do you stand on this? Here's one man's profession:

In a January 1954 letter to the philosopher Eric Gutkind, Albert Einstein (who called himself "a deeply religious nonbeliever") described the idea of God as a "product of human weakness." I might mention this letter was written one year before his death but unearthed only some 50 or so years later. It was auctioned off in London. The anonymous winning bid was $404,000, 25 times the pre-sale estimate! Someone obviously thought highly of Einstein's documented thinking.[3] Mr. Einstein's comment here, "a product of human weakness," poses one answer to the question raised above: did we simply invent this idea of God, possibly out of a sense of its utility to counter our weakness? Or, is there a more enigmatic wisdom at work here? Might it be what we call God? Let's see if we can peek behind the curtain here, so to speak.

Is there really a difference between the idea of God, and the existence of God? Absolutely. If we cannot first conceive of God, how can we possibly suppose God's existence? Well, some can't; most don't stop to think about such a question. Most simply accept that "God exists," or "God is real." We call this faith. But does faith prove anything? Oh my; what a challenging question! Let's look at this a bit.

Absent anything expanding that statement of faith, that God exists, it's what we call but a coherent abstraction, or notion. You may say you believe it; it's a concept (God's existence) that can be imagined, but as it stands, it's only something that can be imagined, not necessarily representing or revealing something real. At its most basic meaning, that's what the idea of God is, a coherent abstraction. But, perhaps both the individual and collective imagined is sufficient upon which to consider the reality of God. How so?

Per above, the idea of God fulfills three very basic personal human needs, or wants: protection, perfection and perpetuity. Absent the possibility of God, which in our thinking represents power (to protect), perfection (to correct), and immortality (to give hope), man until recently has had little to look forward to here on this third rock from the sun. Historically, human progress was slow. In the West, man and society cowered in a static world and world conditions of intimidation, want, and probably despair for centuries. If that does not make holding the idea of God—or something akin to the idea of God—a reality, at a minimum it makes the idea of God (hope) a human necessity simply to endure. That in itself represents an intellectual reality, a truth.

How do we go about demonstrating the certainty of this claim? In modern times, more and more would probably agree it's unlikely to be found, or at least exclusively relied upon, in biblical revelation as that has come down to us today.

We talk a lot about what's real, what is true, and how we know, if in fact we do or can know. So the question: do we or can we know…anything? Well, let's see (we're going to get a bit linguistically technical for a spell here).

First, we need to define reality. What is reality? Reality is the conjectured, or presumed state of things as they actually exist; a postulate, or fact. Simply put, reality is a fact based upon the evidence. It is that which underlies and is the verity of appearances or phenomena rather than as they may appear or might be imagined, whether or not they are observable or comprehensible.[4] The truth refers to what is conjecturably (a term we will define in a moment) real.

That makes perfectly reasonable sense to me, and it's in this context that I'll use these terms. However, there are those who would disagree with me on the clearness, neatness, all-inclusiveness and logical validity of such a simple straight forward statement of "fact." In other words, an issue (problem) is that we often cannot (do not) all agree on what is real or truthful. Welcome, as they say, to the "real (authentic, genuine, somewhat subjectively objective) world."

So, okay, what difference does such possible disagreement make? Individually, probably not much, assuming a minimum degree of tolerance, like live and let live. Collectively (socially and culturally), potentially a lot more. Why? Because it involves world views and our collective understanding of the world around us and governs our collective way of life. At the level of society, religious belief (truths held) influences cooperation, mutual respect, solidarity, a sense of identity and the basis for a collective morality and authority in the society.[5]

While everyone is entitled to his or her own opinions, they are not entitled to their own facts. Facts are actualities (what's real). Facts are empirical, demonstrable or show objective existence and thus represent truth, reality. In some cases, strong conviction in our individual views (opinions) of reality and truth lead us to accept and proclaim some of these (opinions) as "fact." They are not facts, or truth, as defined herein. But admittedly, they can be strongly, and even widely held. Bottom line here, societal agreement or disagreement on what is real or truthful can be highly influential, for better or for worse.

Fortunately, in Western cultures since what has been termed the English and French Enlightenments of the eighteenth century, a reasonable degree of tolerance has developed such that our opinions and faux-facts have not been a cause for ultra-discrimination or persecutions. There have been exceptions over the years, but generally an atmosphere of live and let live has developed. So, if this is the case, what's the issue here? Where am I going with this? I'm going to the question of God as reality, as truth within the confines of the definition of reality and truth herein. Why? Because, as a freethinker, I'm seeking alternative answers to issues such as this. Maybe you are too.

What do I expect (hope) to gain? Some degree of clarity, perhaps even comfort, regarding an eons-long contentious question. First whether God is indeed "real," or secondly at a minimum, whether the conception, "the idea of God," provides a reality. Directly, the first objective seems remote. If, however, the idea of God itself can be demonstrated to be a reality, if this is the case, then is God true by implication?

By "God," I mean the monotheistic biblical deity considered the Supreme Entity, Creator and Ruler of the universe.[6] In times now mostly past in the West, the reality of such a God was all but unquestioned. Today many neither embrace nor believe in such a God. Liberalism and progress, as the primary result of science—leading to an improvement in the human condition—they say, has undermined the theological foundations of such a deity. Is that really the case?

Theology is the field of study, thought and analysis that treats of God; it is the science or study of divine things or what are referred to as religious truths. Modern day science is a branch of knowledge or study of facts or truths systematically arranged and showing the operation of general laws, i.e., systematized knowledge. It encompasses especially knowledge of the physical and material world. Throughout modern history—say from the fifteenth century—science has made an immense impression on the general public. Looking back, we see every department of thought gradually revolutionized under the influence of the discoveries of science. The Medieval approach of aiming at the discovery of divine purpose in the phenomena of nature has been abandoned. Theology has been forced to withdraw everything that it had taught of the material universe.[7] When referring to "theology" I'm referring primarily to Christian teachings.

Does this mean that theology/religion was (is) wrong? Well, as about the material universe, yes obviously. But it was wrong only from the standpoint of accepting appearances often consistent with belief then apparently supported by revelation—see following paragraph. Guilty of conclusions from self-serving observation. It suffered from a lack of knowledge and a reluctance to question, based upon the times; of beliefs (opinions) presented as facts, which science subsequently, if slowly, unveiled that contradicted the teaching of revealed truth about the universe. Nobody likes to be proven wrong and theologians are certainly no exception.

Formal religion retreated from its astronomical teachings based on long held belief in biblically revealed "truth" reluctantly, to say the least, as the new scientific findings threatened many of the basic tenets of faith in their God. The history of the Catholic Church's position on Galileo is a prime example, both of the Church's then (early 17ᵗʰ century) position on scripturally supported "facts" and its slow retreat from its original position over the next few hundred years.

At the time of its original 17ᵗʰ century position in favor of Aristotelian geocentrism (the earth is the center of the universe) it has been expressed that the Church, at the time, kept much more closely to accepted reason than did Galileo himself. And it prudently took into consideration the ethical and social consequences of Galileo's contrary teaching. Its position moderated over the next 250 years, but it was only in 1992 that then Pope John Paul II publicly exonerated (kind of) Galileo (who for some time we had known had it right) by stating that the error of the theologians of the time when they maintained the centrality of the Earth was to think that our understanding of the physical world's structure was, in some way, imposed by the literal sense of sacred scripture. This was hardly an apology; more of a rationalization that put Galileo in a more favorable light while justifying the then action of the Church. As I say, the times make the difference.

An interesting (to me) modern day side-story that suggests parallels to the historically chastening Church experience with the Galileo affair is the case of the Belgian theologian Jacques Dupuis (1923 – 2004). His 1997 book "*Toward a Christian Theology of Religious Pluralism*" sought to reconcile the doctrine that only Christ brings salvation for mankind with a pluralism that sees the possibility of salvation through other religions. (Uh oh!) In 2001 his book led to Dupuis being investigated by the Congregation for the Doctrine of the Faith. The Congregation (aka the C.D.F.), a department of the Roman Curia, was founded to defend the Church from Heresy. Its sole objective is to spread sound Catholic doctrine and defend those points of Christian tradition which seem in danger because of new and unacceptable doctrines.[8]

The C.D.F. noted "ambiguities" regarding agreement between what Dupuis called a "Christian theology of religious pluralism" and the teaching of the Second Vatican Council. Dupuis was told to clarify his position in relation to that document, but, unlike Galileo, he was never formally disciplined. Future editions of his book had to include a copy of the Congregation's notification about areas in which it considered his work unclear.

It's only supposition, but a case might be made that the Church was reluctant to set up a situation paralleling the Galileo affair where somewhere down the line they would have to again face public scrutiny and issues of changed world/religious circumstances, perhaps with the future understanding of Universalism, of "God's plan of salvation of mankind." There is general agreement among friends and colleagues that "the ordeal he went through with the C.D.F. had caused havoc to his mental and physical health." Dupuis died a few days after celebrating 50 years of priesthood, in Rome. He was 81.[9]

Theology to this day will still claim that while science may explain the how (again, the horizontal truth), it does not, and cannot, explain the purpose and why of creation (the vertical truth). Some maintain that science is wrong and hold to the biblically revealed truth about the material universe. They represent an element that will not, perhaps cannot, accept reality, the "facts"—the conjectured state of things. Their faith in the revealed word of the Bible and of institutional preaching about God is that strong. Others less fundamental admit to the findings of science for the most part, but continue to hold "beliefs" that contradict facts, or highly probable natural conclusions, as they exist today. Evolution is a prime example. So, if science has not won the battle for men's minds, it has certainly established a broad beachhead against retreating appearing conservative Western monotheistic theologies.

There are certainly some things science is not able to explain, but the list of them in the physical world appears shrinking. It seems certain that science is not soon going to cause theology and popular religion to disappear. Nor do I believe it necessarily wants to. Nonetheless its findings are a challenge to belief, to faith in the supernatural in the West. Can these two fields of belief and knowledge be reconciled, in the sense of ceasing to be hostile or in opposition to each other?

On the theological side, many think they can. However, they seem to be defending from a weakened position under present conditions.[10] Nonetheless, science has so far not proven the non-existence of God (or the fallacy of the idea of God). All it has demonstrated is that, in all probability, based upon empirical evidence, the God of the Bible was not a necessity in the process of creation of the world and the appearance/evolution of life upon this world. Still, that seems a big hit for religion.

I want to shift gears a bit here now and focus for a moment on how one reads the Bible. Specifically, on the figural interpretation of what it says as opposed to a literal reading of what it purports to say. It's relevant to our consideration of the idea of God vs. god.

The theological creation-myths are pretty clearly just that, myths handed down over time that provided an acceptable explanation (understanding) of creation to the peoples of the ancient Near East at that time. And, of course, they empowered theology. They provided the basis for a figural interpretation, as opposed to the literal word of the Bible. That is, they provided a way of reading in which the biblical text has a second level of meaning. One that pertains to another metaphysical or temporal order of reality, distinct from the reality of the here and now. Figural interpretation of the Bible by an enlightened few led to the development of two significant theological eventualities.

Reading the Bible figuratively claimed to reveal a perfect/divine world that exists (1) either in the near future, when God will utterly transform the material world (eschatology), or (2) in a spiritual plane that is beyond the material world (Platonism). These future "divine worlds" became relevant to the masses (in the here and now) since, theologians insisted, one must reorder one's life in accordance with right belief. Proper religious practice was theologically ordained necessary in order to experience this power of mortal transformation—life everlasting, perpetuity. With the gift of spiritual (biblical) interpretation, the Word becomes a secret window onto the hidden world to come, which holds salvation for those who can perceive it and who can change their lives according to its precepts, i.e. "believe."[11]

This was a theological presentation that became dominant in Western culture for nearly two millennia, from roughly 300 BCE to about 1,600 CE. In abridged form, it persists in many circles until the present day. But with the passage of time and the benefit of accumulated knowledge and general democratization/liberalization of Western cultures, these second (cryptic) levels of biblical meaning have come into question, increasingly so since the Protestant Reformation. The pendulum, as they say, since the Reformation has swung sharply in the other direction, that is of literalism. As an apparent result of this "progress" at least the Christian religion in the developed Western societies is losing adherents.

As mentioned earlier, in the United States between 1990 and 2013 the proportion of Americans who identify as Christians declined nationally from 86 percent to 71 percent; in the North East, the decline was to 64 percent. And this apparent trend is not limited to the US. Between 2001 and 2011, English Christians declined by some 5.3 million members. At this rate, by 2067 there will be no more Christians left in England. Across the USA and in Western Europe, hundreds of empty churches.[12] Does this decline in the religiosity of people equate to the belief that God isn't? Not necessarily. Note that the decline mentioned above was in regard to "Christians," not to a held belief in God, or the idea of God. Nonetheless, subsequent research indicates the numbers for God-believers is declining as well.[13]

The late American mythologist Joseph Campbell said that myths guide us through time and the trials of life; God is a manifestation of the mind [a coming into being, or evidence]. Divinity is what we think— the idea; faith—the subjective reality—is what we experience.[14] If this be the case, then the decline in religious identification and church attendance as evidenced earlier is no doubt due in some part to the nature of the experience of faith in the Church today, versus our thoughts about divinity, be those thoughts considered orthodox by the religious establishment or not. At least in the West, the Christian myth is apparently not serving many of us well today as we "move through time and the trials of life."

Campbell, were he still alive today (he died in 1987), would argue that today Western man has no myths to guide him. Myths need time to develop. As the Christian myth has increasingly been exposed to question, our times, according to Campbell, are moving too fast for new ones to develop and be considered. When change is a constant, there is little if any quiet water in a fast running river. At best, all you can do is to "hold on." For some of us, this is apparently proving difficult.

I spoke above of no one wanting to be proven wrong. The same can be said for most of us not wanting to be considered different. In an editorial on the decline in the nation's Christian population in the periodical *The Christian Century,* it stated that considering the fact that mainline Protestants and Catholics declined in parallel fashion indicates that a wider cultural phenomenon (change) is taking place. "Christian belief and churchgoing are and will be increasingly countercultural"[15] (This echoes comments from the pulpit in my own church recently). To me that means "different" and few, especially the young, want to be perceived as different. Karen Armstrong in the final chapter of her 1993 book *A History of God* highlighted that for 4,000 years the idea of God has constantly adapted to meet the demands of the present, but in our own century, more and more people have found that it no longer works for them, and when religious ideas cease to be effective they fade away.[16]

A reasonable conclusion, at least here in the West, is thus that the monotheistic religion(s) out of the past—or at least Christianity—need to adapt if they are to continue to be considered relevant as in times past. God knows (no pun intended) many seem to be trying. Across the USA, according to Carol Howard Merritt, author of *Tribal Church*, seminary graduates often complain their degrees prepare them for congregations that existed fifty years ago.[17] The religious experience has to be meaningful to the divine thought. It seems that when human beings contemplate the Absolute they have very similar ideas and experiences. The sense of presence, ecstasy and dread in the presence of a perceived reality seems to be a state of mind and a perception that are natural and endlessly sought by human beings.[18] Perhaps Pope Francis's recent observation that "church leaders . . . who stubbornly try to recover a past that no longer exists have a static and inward-directed view of things, and have turned faith into ideology" is worth considering as part of the problem of following in the broader Church today.[19]

So, after some meandering here, you might reasonably ask how does all this point to the reality of God; that God, or at least the idea of such a God—as defined here—is "true" (again, divinity is what we *think*; faith is what we *experience*)? Recall we defined reality as the "conjectured state of things" as they *actually exist* rather than as they may appear or might be imagined. "Conjecture" is the formation of a consensus (best guess) about things as they are without sufficient evidence for complete proof. In that sense, they are contingent upon the type and amount of evidence available upon which to base a conclusion. Most would define the results of science in this manner.

Thinking combined with the understanding of what existence means are the key links in all this. The difference between opinion and concluded fact is the amount and quality of evidence in support of its "reality." Call it probability: the ability to probably prove or probably disprove a proposition, over and over and over again.

Thinkers both great and not so great, ancient and modern, have made a distinction between (1) thoughts corresponding to reality—as defined below, (2) coherent abstractions (thoughts of things that are imaginable but questionably real), and (3) that which cannot even be rationally thought. Reality is most often restricted solely to that which has physical existence *or* has a direct basis in it in the way that thoughts do in the brain (patriotism, for example). Reality is often contrasted with what is imaginary, delusional—only in the mind—dreams, what is false or fictional or what is abstract. Note that both the existence and reality of abstractions is philosophically in dispute. One school regards them as mere words; another regards them as representing higher truths than less notional concepts—welcome, again, to the real world.

At the same time, however, what is abstract plays a role in both everyday life and in academic pursuit. For example, causality, virtue, life, distributive justice (and patriotism) are abstract concepts that can be difficult to define, but they are only rarely equated with pure delusion. While both the existence and reality of abstractions may be in dispute, most accept the utility of them as part of a world view of how we think and arrange our lives in society, at least unconsciously.

Truth, while not a relative term (believe it or not), has a contingent meaning associated with it. That is, upon how we construct what we are referring to. The phrase, "that's a tall mountain" is true, if by tall we understand "tall" as being about 1,000 feet high. If tall is defined as being three to five thousand feet high (the conjectured state), it is not true. Personal opinion does not change truth which is contingent upon context. Whether or not you accept something as true only reflects how you, the individual, is aware of and understands the context, or fail completely to grasp such a contingency concerning an abstract notion. You may believe it; it's a concept, an idea (of God, in our case), that can be imagined. However, as it stands, it's only something that can be imagined. It does not necessarily represent or reveal something real. But even so, perhaps the imagined is sufficient upon which to consider the reality of God. Again, how so?

Abstractions are rarely dismissed as pure delusion. They also represent ideas that are at least humanly imaginable. If they didn't, we would apparently not be able to even think them. Thus, through the mind we can at least conceive of the concept, the idea, of God. That concept, that enduring intellectual object of thought, itself is sufficient upon which to construct belief (in the concept) and once so constructed, to have some degree of faith in such a belief. Recall, divinity is what we think; faith is what we experience. Does that all make it "true" or is such an abstract "belief"—while imaginable— still a fiction? I'm thinking that in this particular case, it really doesn't matter.

Here's an example of why not. The German social theorist, Max Horkheimer (1895-1973), saw God as an important ideal (what I referred to above as perfection). Whether God existed or not, or whether we believed in God, was superfluous. Without the idea of God—perfection in this case—there is no absolute meaning, truth or morality. Ethics becomes simply a question of tastes, a mood or a whim. Unless politics and morality somehow include the idea of "God" (the good) they will remain pragmatic and shrewd rather than wise. If there is no absolute there is no reason that we should not hate, or that war is worse than peace.[20]

Thus, what matters is that we, individually or collectively, can form and retain the coherent idea of the good, of God; that "God exists," or "God is real." Permit me to repeat that: what matters is that we, individually or collectively, can form and retain the coherent idea of the good, of God. That idea, or conception, may only exist in our minds—individually or collectively—but in our minds it represents an individualized conjectured state of things as they actually are, in our minds, i.e. what we think. Does that make this idea of God true, as we have defined it? Does this make God a reality, as we have defined it?

As for the god of the idea, no, unfortunately, it doesn't. Not by these standards—standards established by human beings to rationally define reality and the truth as we human beings employ these terms. Why not? Because the quantity and quality of the evidence in support of our individual belief is insufficient to establish the reality or truth of God beyond our faith in this coherent idea. Regrettably we are forced to use these man-made intellectual tools in attempting to confirm the object of a concept, even a need, which is in all its meaningfulness to us questionably definable in the first place by rational human argument. Damn!

Nonetheless, this failure to establish a truth of God by human standards does not diminish *the reality of the idea of God* as a broad if not universal need for such idea. Thus, we seem to be left with the fact of a reality, even a necessity, which is unsupported by what we call truth. Ironic. But, maybe there is more regarding "truth" to be considered here.

Hold on, someone is going to say. The only thing you have demonstrated here is that the idea of God is a widely-held opinion.

And as you yourself pointed out (on page 48) opinions can be both widely and strongly held, but that does not make them facts. That's right, it doesn't. And I have already conceded that holding the idea of God does not in and of itself make the god of the idea a fact, an objective reality.

Nevertheless, the idea of God seems clearly an individualized "conjectured state of things" as they actually exist—in the mind. The sheer quantity of individuals around the world who hold this conjectured state of things in their minds (in all religions) as well as the manner in which most externally express the idea seems sufficient evidence (in quantity and quality) to confer upon the idea the pragmatic reality I give it. And keep in mind the apparent human recognition (need) for the nonmaterial as well as the material in life in some combination—call it the psychological if you like—dictates that what might be considered a double standard of determining "truth" or "existence" is neither unrealistic nor bending the existing rules here.

Recall I also pointed out (on page 55) that reality is most often restricted solely to that which has (a) physical existence <u>or</u> (b) has a direct basis in it in the way that thoughts do in the brain (patriotism, for example). The idea of God has, in my analysis, such a direct basis in it. I stand by my conclusion in this regard.

Slightly changing focus (again!), I want to take up the issue of just how the god of the idea is conceptualized for us.

Religion in the West has anthropomorphized (humanized) if not the idea of God the vision of God. It's an understandable attempt to make God as humanly user-friendly as possible while retaining a preferred position of interpretation and intercession between man and his personal idea of God. In so doing, it has in its mortal endeavor and position of authority dumbed-down the idea of God for the masses to a "superhuman" understanding; a being, not unlike ourselves; a "Living God" ("Our Heavenly Father") in an anthropomorphic sense. It has incarnated God into human form in the person of Jesus of Nazareth, humanly creating for mortal representation what is in actuality a divine aseity, an underived or independent existence: "The Word Became Flesh."

It has promoted a god in our own image—recall that the Book of Genesis, for example, is the product of at least four human authors or redactors over some four hundred years—for our own earthly purposes. It has developed and promoted it, offering this humanly understandable vision of God in exploitation of the need that the idea of God is based upon: our human frailty, imperfection and mortality. We obviously badly need a god that can help us overcome. And if not overcome to at least make the perceived burden of such human failings and limitations lighter as we move through life. But in all this well-intended endeavor religion has not in the millennia it has tried come anywhere closer to demonstrating the reality and truth of the idea of God, or God, than has the rational argument above. A mystery is what it purports to deals with; hope is the only prescription it offers.

As we have witnessed over the centuries, the existence of such a god has been neither humanly provable nor unprovable (maybe the Positivists are right). Of what good is a god of such an ambiguous, equivocal profile, other than to sooth our own personal, egotistic earthly and mortal concerns and beg it to give us each day our daily needs? As Frederick A. Niedner, professor and associate director of the Institute of Liturgical Studies at Valparaiso University put it, "Sometimes it seems as if we unwittingly treat God like some kind of cosmic concierge or super Siri who stands ready to do our bidding, whether we are praying about misplaced files and crucial ball games or cancer cures and climate change."[21] This is a view of God that selfishly serves us. We have emasculated this God such that while we may still give lip service to its omniscience, omnipresence and (possibly) omnipotence, it is looked upon more as our servant. By paying it homage, or at least lip service, God's presumptive largess and grace, and in the end our salvation, become an entitlement.

Like the German-Jewish public intellectual and religious philosopher Herman Cohen (1848 – 1919) and others, I'm disinclined to believe, or to accept, that God is a being, an external reality that imposes Its will from on high. God—the idea of God—represents a mortal aspiration; simply an essential, I repeat, an essential idea formable by the human mind, a symbol of the ethical ideal. There is an idea corresponding to every general conception we have, such as love, justice and beauty. The highest of all is the idea of the good, or God (according to Plato). Spinoza, in his attempt to prove God, said "the very idea of 'God' contains a validation of God's existence..."[22] This seems but a form of the old Ontological Proof for God's existence, but it reinforces the point that it is the "idea of God" that is significant.

The external reality of such a God does not follow from this, but the individual conception, the idea, gives rise to the divinity of our thoughts. This in turn allows the belief—the human experience of the divine—to exist. Thus, within this context, "God exists," or "God is real." Abstractly then, God is true on both a personal and perhaps even a collective level.

In support of this, recall we said reality is most often restricted solely to that which has a physical existence *OR* has a direct basis in it in the way that thoughts do in the brain. This may equate to God being reduced to nothing (No-Thing) from a Western anthropomorphic vision as a Super-Being somewhere "out there;" The Old Man in the Sky—think Michelangelo's painting, *The Creation of Adam, or the Wizard of Oz behind the curtain*—directing the activities of the universe from on high, but historically that appears to be the "reality," or truth of the matter: God is No-Thing. To paraphrase René Descartes' famous dictum, "I think therefore I am," we might say, God is because we can—and maybe even need to—think God is.

The simple idea of God, simply conceived—the idea—represents divinity. Belief in the need-based reality of our idea of God is therefore what we experience: faith; faith in an idea we can conceive and retain, even if for many somewhat skeptically. Does that make it a reality? (Is patriotism a reality?) It may well, under our definition of reality, for most of humanity.

Then, what of religion? What part has and does it play in belief and faith? How necessary is it? On an individual basis, religiosity is essentially an inner feeling—the idea—that there is a God, and this is promoted by the Church. Religion, the institution, is a man-made enterprise. Organized religion is an attempt to channel belief (of the idea of God) into more of a conformed corporate expression of the divine nature and bring about a discipline of how to approach the object of our thought for maximum human advantage. It likewise demands certain observances as well as respect for its/your god. A danger of institutional religion, however, is that it can become an end in itself as opposed to a means to an end.

Each of today's three God-based religions is guided in its approach to belief and encouraging faith by revealed information about, and ostensibly from, its god by divine revelation. As humanity and its societies and cultures have moved (hopefully mostly forward) through the centuries, new information, earthly discoveries and accumulated knowledge have brought into question much of this revealed word, from both an exegetical and a mortal point of view. There are other more reasonable explanations for many matters that were once seen explained only by religious teaching, based upon revelation. Look carefully here and you may detect a long-term trend.

The trend I and no doubt others see in the West is one on a lessening of the reliance on organized religion for divine intercession and instruction, as well as a shift in emphasis away from the historical idea of God. The Reformation was certainly an early example of this. We have noted the decline in religious affiliations in the West. That seems a logical result. Modernity has seen an improvement in both the quality and quantity of life for many on earth. Public indications are this is continuing, albeit at an uneven pace in places around the world. Again, we refer to it as "progress."

By progress I mean improvement in the human condition. Many, if not most today, would attribute this improvement not—at least directly—to God but to hopeful evolution in the institutions of man under which we live. The rule of law and a better understanding of natural phenomena, and how to deal with it, lessens the supplication to God for protection. Ethics, compassion and an improving sense of justice practiced by more makes the possibility of correction (perfection) closer to hand. This perceived optimism leads many to minimize the idea of God as a primary prerequisite for progress in favor of a do-it-ourselves capability well within the human experience, humanism, if you will. Under such circumstances, the need for a traditional religious idea of God recedes in the human consciousness. Does this make the idea of God less a reality? I doubt it; just less of an awareness. This I would suggest is one area the Church needs to ponder. I return to the thoughts of Herr Horkheimer above. Perhaps a greater consideration of such thinking by the Church would be of practical religious value.

In the Church's corner, however, is an apparent truism: while the idea of God yields an ethical and self-serving ideal, it's difficult to sustain belief in an absolutely abstract concept. Belief is sustained and promoted by the familiar and by an emotional connection in life. The Church and its presentation of the god of the idea is, still today, probably still best suited to accommodate these needs for most.

Immortality: the biggest most delicious carrot for human consumption the Church has to offer. Can it really be? Well, I guess that depends upon how you define it. The Church admits we die, but somehow holds to the idea that this does not represent death, at least for those who believe according to the Church. Some in medicine do not, in my understanding, rule out the existence of a soul or other non-corporeal human attribute (consciousness) that might survive bodily death—based primarily upon reports of "near-death experiences"—but more and more seem to be questioning the basis for "a next world," at least as we have been religiously led to believe.

For most, I would think, immortality means continued consciousness, some continuation of what we experience in our mortal lives. If not, of what relevance might it be to us? The First Law of Thermodynamics (conservation of energy) states that in a closed system matter or its energy equivalent can neither be created nor destroyed. Although that principle dates from the eighteenth century, I have never heard it brought up in modern Christian theology. Therefore, I assume this is not their idea of "life everlasting," immortality. It certainly isn't mine. But basing the concept largely on the purported experience of one single human individual and a few letters of an itinerant zealous Jewish evangelist named Paul seems a questionable basis to offer the same experience or expectation to millions (and millions) of others. Especially since, to my knowledge, this occurrence has never been successfully repeated. For many, the concept of everlasting life (as we know it) in the context of what we know about material organics, of which we are one, seems increasingly unlikely. Therefore, the carrot of potential immortality, based solely upon hope is apparently not a sufficient motivator to pursue at the moment. What a pity.

Nonetheless, despite all this says in my understanding, religion as we experience it today is not about to disappear from the scene. Its role and emphasis may evolve; may change. As and if man's ability to continue to progress—call it humanism as above described—moves forward the classical role of religion will in all probability continue to be in question: "who needs it?" As pointed out above, when religious ideas cease to be effective, they fade away. But, who knows? Hope is a tough human attribute to dim. I still play the lottery from time to time in spite of the odds!

Given all the above, it's not inconceivable that—as I broached the possibility earlier—the Bible does have it backwards: man may well have stumbled upon (created) the idea of God. But I contend the utility of the idea justifies it. It's a good idea, and in the end just where the idea originated is not as important as having it. Mankind being such as he/she is, it might also be that humanity cannot be humanity as it has come to be, absent this idea. As such, while the idea may evolve over time to meet our needs, I can't see it disappearing from the human consciousness any time soon. Again, that may not make the god of the idea an objective truth, but it certainly seems to make that god a necessary human reality.[22]

Let's take our examination of this "reality" to the next level.

Chapter Six

The Purpose of God

As I suggested in the prologue, this was one of the two questions I asked myself as I pondered my belief in the Judeo-Christian presentation of God: what is the purpose of God (at least from man's viewpoint)—the "why" of God? It might seem we covered this in the last chapter—the three P's of protection, perfection and perpetuity—but here we want to get much more specific. I mean here, by the purpose of God, more the enterprise of God. What does the Christian God of the idea do, or supposed to do, at least according to what we have been taught to understand?

Does special revelation, i.e., God's biblical self-presentation, inform us of this or at least give us some hint? If it doesn't, I for one don't know where else to seek an answer. I'm convinced that biblical revelation, as interpreted by the Church, does provide the answer and I'll share it with you. I doubt you will be surprised by the revelations, but may be with my conclusion.

For anyone who is a "believer" this may seem a strange or unnecessary subject. For those who have determined that belief is self-deception, a chimera, it will seem a waste of time. For what may be a considerable number of us somewhere between the peace of belief and the vacuity of disbelief, I suspect my pursuit here will receive sympathetic consideration. My own personal situation (as most will recognize by now) is one of seeking and finding the path not only long and arduous but almost impossible to make out at times.

Obstructions across the path, such as this question of the purpose of God, seem to be put there to hinder my progress; to make me question my goal of assured belief supported by a strong faith. As I have suggested, I can no longer even make out the outlines of a path.

The chapter title here is primarily a question, i.e., what is the "why" of God? This may seem a misnomer. I might seem to be asking what the essence of God is. But essence doesn't quite correspond with what I seek here. Essence means the basic or necessary constituent of something; its intrinsic nature as contrasted with what is accidental, ephemeral or superficial. It seems highly unlikely that I, or any mortal, could know or understand the essence of God. As the earlier quoted Father of Modern Philosophy René Descartes put it a few hundred years back, "...tis contrary to reason that the less perfect should give rise to the more perfect." On the other hand, I suppose if we did know it, or of it, that might make human understanding of the god of the idea easier. It's a thought, but not one I'll pursue further here in my quest for getting a handle on the purpose of God.

The tendency in searching for answers is too often to go back to the beginning and raise the question—yet another time—does the god of the idea exist? I think most who have come this far would agree, "been there; done that." My expressed position is that the god of the idea is a necessary human reality. Even atheists need a god to deny. For the purpose at hand I accept that as a general rule belief in God is consciously based not on objective fact (or the worldly or contemporary conjectured state of things), but on faith, as a result of the divine idea; that disbelief is based not on fact but on lack of faith. I recognize that this makes any conclusion I draw here contingent on faith, or lack thereof, and I accept that condition.

But the nature of God, as perceived, seems to demand consideration before we can speak of any purpose of It. Admittedly, this too is contingent and accepted as such. By God's understood (Christian) nature, whether intrinsic or not, God is omnipotent, or all powerful. God is omniscient, all knowing and creating; omnipresent; one enjoying sovereignty over all, everywhere, for all time. God is eternal, outside of time—always has been and always will be. God is singular, in the triune Christian sense, and represents unity. That last one is a toughie, kinda hard to clearly grasp: singular in a triune sense.

By such description, it would seem that nothing is beyond God's reach, power or understanding. And from this that all things, occurrences and events can be explained satisfactorily by Godly design, or intent, and thus owe their existence or occurrence to God, directly or indirectly. It follows from such a nature that all things can be, and have been, attributed to God.

The question is, as finite man's worldly knowledge and experience have expanded and accumulated over time—lots of time—is this divine nature still universally understood and accepted among Christians? Or, as I have suggested, has man's view—but not the Church's—of the biblical God's nature and stature changed?

To reiterate, my layman's answer to this question is that where we once looked to the god of the idea as the reason, cause or basis for many earthly and even non-earthly matters not otherwise humanly explainable, direct divine reliance is no longer an absolute or necessary explanation. We think we have non-divine explanations for previously unanswerable questions; we believe we have figured out, based primarily on earthly evidence and experience, matters previously understood solely upon the nature and/or enterprise of God. It may be described as learning, as ignorance or misunderstanding overcome. Historically, either by God's silence or apparent absence from the scene, this perception of man's intellectual progress seems divinely unchallenged.

In gaining this experience and understanding of earthly matters, it has increased man's self-confidence and shrunk our reliance on and understanding of the scope of God's proclaimed involvement to some degree. God may (optimistically) still be viewed as omnipotent, omniscient and omnipresent, but perhaps not quite to the degree as in times now past, and by fewer people. This being the situation, the current understanding of the nature of God, then we can turn to the question of the purpose of the god of the idea in this light.

WHAT DOES GOD DO? Considering our (my) understanding

of the Christian nature of God *today,* if asked to list the ten most apparent responsibilities or functions—purpose—of God, based primarily upon special revelation (the Bible), what would they be? Let's see if my imperfect knowledge can come up with these, in no special order:

- Offer grace (unmerited favor; a form of mercy)
- Provide forgiveness (a reward for repentance)
- Guarantee salvation (extend life eternally)
- At some point, judge the wicked and the good (a potential of justice)
- Give spiritual guidance (a signpost for rightful mortal living)
- Create (provide order out of chaos)
- Offer hope (encourage optimism)
- Promote love (teach that peace is preferable to strife)
- Instill charity (infuse a sense of thankfulness)
- Impress fear (remind us of the fact of consequences)

These, biblically, would seem to be at least the primary functions of God, as understood, with which man is familiar.

Combine all these in one "pot," stir to blend, and the purpose of the god of the idea would appear—not unreasonably—to be to provide us humans a combined sense of security, optimism and comfort to off-set the insecurities, pessimism and discomforts with which mortal life too often confronts us. This is certainly consistent with and reinforces that which the idea of God represents, protection, perfectibility and perpetuity. One might even describe this as providing a sense of psychological balance in life. In Christian parlance it's boiled down and referred to as "hope," personified in the incarnate Christ. Hope in the return of Christ is the basis for believers to purify themselves in this life. [1]

Is hope simply wishful thinking? Generally speaking, yes it is. But when you fortify hope with belief, and faith in support of belief, it becomes something more. The biblical definition of hope is "confident expectation." Hope so supported becomes a firm assurance regarding things that are unclear and unknown.[2] The difficulty of relying upon hope, absent any further evidence or collateral is that it is little more than accepting the injunction, "Trust me."

Admittedly this view of purpose minimizes the more traditional understanding that the "blessings of God" may only be validated at a projected future day of judgment—something to look forward to in the here-after. My lay-conclusion here looks worldly, at the here and now, though it seems true that much of the way the Christian message is delivered is akin to a carrot before the horse; to motivate us to work towards a personal future beyond the here and now. Still, the end effect seems the same, to offer hope, support, and comfort in the here and now where it is needed, for those who need it.

Is this conclusion of God's purpose consistent with both the Hebrew text and New Testament of the Bible? That is, is the purpose of the God of the Jews the same as the purpose of the God of Christians? I detect a difference.

The original divine purpose for the Jews seems to have been to dictate structure and provide community guidance through a covenantal relationship with an at-risk tribal society. Can we reconcile the threatening God of the Books of Genesis, Job or the Prophets with the loving God of the Gospel of John, or the epistles of Paul and Peter and James? This seems a formidable challenge. If nothing else, the character or focus of God's purpose, as per the above, seems to have shifted from the earlier group emphasis (God's Law) to the later individual emphasis (God's Love), biblically.

How important is the evolving nature of knowledge compared to historical divine guidance (special revelation) for now pretty well structured cultures of Western society? Are covenantal relationships (treaties between nations considered) even tolerated or welcome any longer in Western cultures? Today most developed Western societies understand the individual as central, at least socially and politically. Cultures change over time, as our knowledge of the world (and universe) we inhabit expands. And yet, in spite of all this evolving within human society, the biblical literalism of traditional (Western) Christianity instructs us to hold onto concepts and understandings of a covenantal religious belief system now over two millennia old. Hold on and believe as if nothing has changed. That's simply not the case. The suggestion of a "New Covenant" with God through Jesus seems, at best, to be unraveling considering the apparent falling away from the faith; at worst it seems one sided, religiously man-made, which negates any divine obligation.

The accumulated knowledge and understanding of earthly events and phenomenon has had major impacts on any number of earlier religious tenets: the earth is not the center of the Universe; the appearance and development of man seems unlikely (all but impossible) to have evolved as we are led to believe in the Bible, even if some thirty-three percent of Americans claim to believe it (per the Pew Research Center). As earlier pointed out, we do know—and can predict—the path of the wind, and just how the body is formed in the mother's womb.[3] These are not minor implications in so far as unchanging "faith" in special revelation is concerned. Nor are they minor in the case of trying to discern the purpose of God (is it primarily for the here and now, or solely aimed at the presupposed here-after?).

If these religious pillars of belief have been discredited, what of others? What of the very core of Christian belief in the promise of the cross: of salvation; of physical resurrection and a personal eternal life based solely on the death and resurrection (itself based significantly on the correct meaning (translation) and understanding of the biblical Greek terms "pistis"—trust/belief, faith/faithfulness; "dikaiosyne"—righteousness; and "charis"—grace)? Ouch!

Finally, on a somewhat more philosophic level, it should be reemphasized that much of Christian tradition is carried out within the legacy of platonic/neo-platonic thought, or influence, even today. In my lay understanding of all this, I suspect this has gotten in the way of Christianity's image of itself in a changing world.

We have inherited the concept of timeless truths (abstract objects) from the classical Greek, from Plato. Truths that exist by themselves—independently—on an ideal plane, perfect in eternity. Here in our world everything is subject to change; nothing is perfect.

In Plato's parallel world (of abstracts), everything is perfect; nothing changes. It was always so, will always be so: Platonic truth exists outside of time. The god of the idea in the (classical Greek) Christian sense represents an abstraction, or what we would call a model, on the infinite plane; the Christian God—the idea—is perfect, existing outside of time, eternal. Man on the other hand is finite; he exists within time, yet Christianity expects mankind to strive to achieve the ideal of a perfect, timeless idea, even if cloaked in a temporary temporal form (The Christ).

This leads to cognitive dissonance:[4] we live in one world while imagining the existence of another; a heavenly plane ("thy will be done on earth as it is in heaven" seems an impossible task, at least for finites). As a result of this paradox, we live in a potential state of alienation from what we may value and strive for. In today's world, traditional Christianity might better consider its insistence on the total dependence of the finite on the infinite in an effort to relieve this cognitive dissonance.

It seems that the Christian God, truths of mathematics and the laws of nature, at least, are endowed with an existence that transcends time. Man, on the other hand, can only act in time but religiously we are urged to judge our actions by God's timeless, perfect standards. The negation of sin and the concept that "God helps those who help themselves" aren't considered proper forms of Christian belief. Is there no "turf" within time wherein God's reign is unconcerned? Is a king of kings in today's understanding really necessary or even properly understood? Only in the Church, it would seem.

It may appear that the implication of these comments is that religion, the Christian religion in this case—but not necessarily the purpose of God—is obsolete or unnecessary. I don't hold to that but do suggest religion suffers from reduced certainty or infallibility by present measures; is no longer as persuasive. One reason for this may well be, some argue, that the way post-Reformation doctrines developed over the past few centuries has left them riddled with inconsistencies and problems. And, by continuing to profess them along with the insistence that the Christian biblical God is immune to finite matters and considerations, although totally involved through finite man, as put forward—and especially post-Reformation Protestant Movements—Christianity has painted itself into a corner. It apparently cannot adapt its model to a changed world.

Does it have to change? Is it religion's responsibility to "keep up?" Yes, in some sense it is if it wishes to be considered relevant. The tree either bends with the wind or it breaks. Unfortunately, it seems too much of today's Christian view of religion finds itself unable to "bend." This is not necessarily a divine issue. The difference between religion and faith is that one is the organizational product of man; the other is not, or at least less so. The Church needs man; man may not need the Church, at least as it exists today.

With the possible exception of tentative liberal Christian post-Enlightenment attempts, it cannot reinterpret, let alone alter, "truths" it has proclaimed for so long. This rigidity, and intractability, has been complicated by the Reformation's view of the absolute inerrancy of the Bible. To propose this to many, if not most, in today's Western culture and society is to display a degree of not only questionable superiority but of disdain of any progress in worldly wisdom, i.e. ignorance, even if benignly displayed. If this conclusion appears to some an example of man's "sinful pride," I do not recognize it as such.

In America at least this has led inevitably to a divergence in the approach, understanding and propagation of Christian religious thinking and demands. The result is a spectrum of belief from the very conservative to the more liberal—to the progressive, actually. It has contributed to the growth of "Spiritualism" and Unitarianism as opposed to traditional Christian belief. Spiritualism in America, per the American Federation of Spiritualist Churches, is a blend of ancient wisdom with contemporary thought. A brief review of their materials would suggest that, in some areas, they have been able to overcome the past and present a God-based religion that seems credible and attractive to the young. Unitarianism is a view of Christian faith that rejects the concept of the Trinity. Universal

71

Unitarians have no creed, and are more in line with Spiritualism or Deism than is Christianity. Some categorize them as humanists.

Humanism in its various forms (I count at least six!) is another faith-based belief system (most without God) that has many adherents. One might wonder if mainline Christianity in its historical efforts to harmonize post-Enlightenment thought with traditional biblical understanding isn't slowly headed in these or similar directions. The expansion of non-traditional Christian belief systems certainly seems to exhibit that people want (need?) something spiritual, or at least non-material, to believe in. This seems so even if that belief system is in themselves, as in humanism. It still represents the spiritual as opposed to the material.

Whether or not liberalism, spiritualism, humanism—or something akin to them—continue to develop to the detriment of traditional conservative Christianity is a question well beyond the scope of this investigation into the purpose of God. But the biblical purpose of God, as put forward here, seems just as comfortable with at least some of the basic beliefs of the more liberal Christian thinking, or even Spiritualism: one offering security, optimism and comfort, as it does for traditional Christian biblical belief, with just the littlest of wiggle-room. From what little I know of humanism, not quite so much.

This gives further credence to the thought—my thought—that in view of the above, the purpose of the Christian god of the idea is to offer comfort and solace in the here and now. If as such, is it of revealed divine origination, or is it an ancient man-made construct to console ourselves in what we saw/see as a discomforting and threatening environment? It would appear to fortify my conclusion that perhaps the Bible does have it backwards: maybe it was man who created the idea of God, rather than mankind being the product of God. That could change quite a lot. For example:

What does the answer to that mean for our promised Christian "salvation"?

That question is way, way above my pay grade…so let's move on!

Entr'acte

My polemical essay regarding the reality of the idea of God is complete. To summarize, if summarization be necessary, the idea of God *is* a human reality, if only subjectively so. It still represents a collective reality, and in that sense an accepted truth. The evidence for this seems beyond question considering the sheer number of individuals world-wide that observe God, in one form or another. In at least the Judeo-Christian sphere, the basis for the idea of God is to provide for the human longing for protection, perfection, and perpetuity in the here and now as opposed to the hereafter. The purpose of the god of the idea is to provide humanity with a supporting sense of security, optimism and comfort to off-set the insecurities, pessimism and discomforts with which mortal life too often confronts us.

It really doesn't matter how we got the idea of God, or if the god of the idea is itself a reality. Having the idea is what counts—it's that good an idea—and provides enormous utility and sustenance for our earthly existence. If there is something beyond mortal life, presently it is unknowable to man. In this sense, Christian hope for an after-life seems little more than wishful thinking, even when fortified with belief and faith. Nonetheless, the idea of God is what I would term prerequisite for a reasonable mortal need for any feeling of emotional or non-material comfort…in the here and now.

However…

To shut down at this point will for many seem to leave the story unfinished; to ignore a presentation of the god of the idea that Christianity developed to bring this idea into a flesh and bones reality—and with no little success admittedly. Almost any Christian will (should) ask, but where do Jesus and the entire "New Testament" figure in the truth here? After all, that scripture is the foundation upon which the Christian Church was built and still stands, even if pretty fractured and somewhat shaky today. Church history is not my target here. But still I agree, the Jesus phenomenon—and I believe that is a good description of it, something that impresses the observer as extraordinary—needs to be considered to round out the story.

So let's consider it.

Chapter Seven

The Jesus Phenomenon

Jesus and the Gospel

If over all the reality of God is a subjective rather than objective truth (conjecture), how are we to understand Jesus, the man who Christians contend was and is for all intents and purposes the god of the idea; both true man and true God? Well, probably not in quite the same way. There is an historical trail to follow in Jesus' case. Jesus' story is time related. It's the iconic story supporting and justifying the Church, although the Church might deny this—that the Church is built upon Jesus, and not upon the god of the idea. The Church would claim there is no difference between the two: Jesus is "God of God, Light of Light; very God of very God; begotten not made, being of one substance with the Father." This, as available history and biblical study demonstrate, seems not immune to question today.

While the god of the idea stands outside of time—certainly aside from its biblical appearances—Jesus is from available evidence historical. Flavious Josephus was a Jewish priest from Jerusalem, a somewhat controversial figure who lived in the first century CE, 37 – 100. He is considered by some our most precious source of Jewish history, religion and culture. He mentions John the Baptist, Jesus and his brother James, if only briefly, in one of his works *Jewish Antiquities* which was written in Rome around the year 90. Some whose career and/or orientation is today religious deplore the pursuit of a historical Jesus as if there were something to fear from this. But if Jesus was truly a man as well as true God (as the Council of Ephesus in 431 specified), there must be a historical side to him that is worth pursuing.

Interest in the historical aspects of Jesus is not a recent pursuit. Almost 200 years ago now, the German liberal protestant theologian and writer David Friedrich Strauss' (1808-1874) 1836 book, *The Life of Jesus, Critically Examined*, "scandalized Christian Europe with its portrayal of the 'Historical Jesus'." And more recently as the late Catholic priest and Biblical scholar Raymond E. Brown pointed out, if Jesus does not have a historical reality, Christianity becomes myth.

For about 1,800 years Christians largely took for granted that the Gospel portrayal of Jesus was a literal factual account of his ministry, and for all practical purposes, his lifetime. Until recently lay-Christians tended to conceive of the first century Jesus movement, eventually resulting in Christianity, as a sort of spontaneous happening (a new covenant). It was thought of as a break with history or new paradigm that changed religious thinking; that Jesus' message and ministry was something new and different, and that people flocked to it simply because it was. Many still do. They believe it basically began with the baptism of Jesus of Nazareth and the biblical celestial pronouncement, "You are my Son, whom I love; with you I am well pleased."[1] Or possibly it was: "This is my Son, whom I love; with him I am well pleased."[2] Take your pick. With this Jesus entered the public domain and began his short public ministry, primarily in and around the villages of the small rural province of Galilee. This is the region where all three synoptic gospels (Matthew, Mark, and Luke) place Jesus' public ministry except for its final days during the Passover festival in Jerusalem.

This presentation is not ahistorical from what we know. But it leaves out a lot of the background upon which the ministry of Jesus was constructed and the Christology developed by the Church in support of its later claims about him.

Sometime around 28-30 CE Jesus was said to be baptized in the Jordan River by the eschatological (the end times) Jew John the Baptizer. John was a charismatic Jewish hermit prophet whose preaching to his fellow Jews was of repentance and purification. He encouraged them to mark their conversion by a ritual immersion, or baptism, in view of the imminently expected arrival of the (Jewish) Kingdom of God. He was described by Josephus in his *Jewish Antiquities* as "a good man who encouraged his compatriots to practice piety towards God, justice among themselves and subject themselves to baptism for the purification of the body, the soul having already been cleansed by righteous behavior."[3]

A connection of John with the earlier (9th century BCE) Jewish prophet Elijah is implicitly alluded to in Mark 1:2 where John is represented in the New Testament as the fulfillment of prophecies of Malachi: "See, I am sending my messenger ahead of you, who will prepare your way." The aim of this new Elijah, we are told, was the proclamation of the impending arrival of God's reign on earth: "Repent, for the kingdom of heaven is at hand." The evangelists (writers of the three synoptic gospels) all see in John the realization of the approach of the Jewish God, the divine King, in the desert as announced in the Book of Isaiah 40:3, 'the voice of one crying out in the wilderness:' "Prepare the way of the Lord, make his paths straight."[4]

I might also mention that the religiously conservative Jewish Qumran community—the Essenes, authors of the Dead Seas Scrolls—choose, relying on Isaiah 40:3, to withdraw to the arid shores of the Dead Sea and return to the divine Law as the ideal condition for preparing for the establishment on earth of the Kingdom of God. This occurred starting about 200 years before Jesus.

The point here is that the historical Jewish Jesus' message was a representation of an existing "religious movement;" he was for all intents and purposes a disciple of John the Baptist and continued his ministry pretty much as his own; it was one of charismatic Judaism with strong eschatological (end of time) orientation. Jesus, simply, was a product of his Jewish times.

He was not a professional theologian who subjected the secret life of God to close scrutiny. He was an existential preacher who endeavored to persuade his disciples to change their lives and to collaborate with him in the great enterprise of preparing the way towards the Kingdom of God.[5] His ministry was in accordance with Jewish thinking, Jewish law, and was aimed specifically at Jews. Although there are conflicting passages in the synoptic gospels, it seems clearly evident from these gospels that Jesus did not have establishing a new or non-Jewish religion as part of either his message or his mission.[6]

In light of the weight of scripture, the final instructions which the apostles are said to have received, "Go therefore and make disciples of all nations, baptizing them in the name of the Father and of the Son and of the Holy Spirit" (reported in Matthew and the longer ending of Mark) are considered highly probably to be later additions by the Church in support of its Gentile evangelizing as opposed to the earlier saying of Jesus.

If this be the case, how did this simple Jewish evangelist Jesus ascend to the position of the god of the idea, God Almighty, in a non-Jewish world-wide religion? The conclusions here seem to suggest that Jesus, following his death, became a role model. He was promoted by others (St. Paul, for example) with originally Jewish backgrounds, as a long anticipated Jewish savior or messiah. As one who, through his death and reputed resurrection, fulfilled Jewish scripture concerning the arrival of the Kingdom of God on Earth; that Jesus in his resurrected (new) life showed the way for others to eternal life. Those (Jews) who believed in him and led a life as instructed by him, could expect life everlasting in the divine realm, Heaven.

That stresses and is consistent with our definition of the idea of God: belief in the Church's Jesus was promoted as offering, at a minimum, perfection and perpetual life, two of the three basic human desires. While within a relatively short time the Jesus movement within Judaism was rejected, it was promoted to the "goyim" successfully, but not without time and great stress and for many persecution for their Christian beliefs and religious practices. It struggled within itself as well as within the Roman Empire until the emperor Constantine decided to act as its patron, not as his predecessors—its enemy—in the early fourth century (312) and it became a legitimate religion of the Empire. Emperor Theodosius II (401-450) made Christianity the official faith of the empire. After this time its rise and influence was steady.

So, what does this non-all-inclusive history of Jesus and early Christianity tell us about Jesus, specifically, and the Church generally? Well, truly, that he was a historical figure. One who by his eschatological understanding of Jewish history dedicated his relatively short public ministry in primarily the "Up-country" of Judea to strict practice of their Torah, preparing Jews to successfully receive the kingdom of God here on earth. His message was directed to Jews. For what have been described as questionable activist activities in the Roman Provence, he was publicly executed (This sort of summary ridding of troublemakers, potential or real, was not uncommon during Roman rule at this time).

While shocked and dismayed by his untimely and from convincing biblical evidence, unexpected execution his close apostles believed they had seen and even spoken with Jesus following his death. They proclaimed him the "risen Messiah," continuing to preach his message of repentance, thereby establishing a "Jesus the Messiah-based" sect within Judaism. This original Jewish "Messiah" sect, led by his brother James, stressed Jesus' teaching over later promoted benefits of his crucifixion and resurrection. These latter are primarily "Pauline" in origin.

Historically for most gentile Christians the meaning of the crucifixion—the cross—is the argument for Christian belief. What is this meaning? That Jesus died for our sins. That God so loved mankind that God dispatched itself in the person of Jesus, God the Son/Logos (in the Trinitarian sense), to our earth specifically to suffer and die as an atonement for the errors of our sinful ways, our sinful natures. We—absolutely everyone—are sinful and deserving of punishment for these sins (I can't really find anything that specific in the Bible itself aside from Paul in Romans 3:23, 5:12-19 and Galatians, 6:8, and possibly 1 Kings 8:46). But God in his love decided to transfer our collective guilt—past, present and future—on to (or in to) the person of the Son Jesus, and to sacrifice his incarnate self as payment (ransom) for our sins. After all, God had biblically promised not to wipe out mankind again after the flood, so what was he to do about his "sinful creations?" This might be interpreted as, "if you can't beat them join them." I mean, talk about a Rube Goldberg approach to a solution for a problem. But, I digress.

Not a bad spot for a digression, because I want to interrupt our train of thought here to consider just how the man Jesus acquired the mantel of the divine. It's relevant, and pretty interesting, I find. I believe we need to understand this as we plunge further into the issue of just how Jesus is presented as our savior and the Church's explanation of how he is going to (or already does) save us.

It's all right there in the New Testament of the Bible. It's really a question of just when, how, and why the divine happened to appear in that finite and particular life. If we can be at all discriminating in reading history, biblical and other, the available evidence would indicate he was certainly not so considered (divine) during his lifetime and ministry. Focus on the following timeline in events pointing to his divine promotion:

The first promoter of Jesus "the Christ" we know of, and the first author of any part of the New Testament, is St. Paul. He antedates the gospels themselves by many years. His writings took place some eighteen to thirty years after the life of Jesus; say in the late 40s and 50s. Listen to his words:

"We preach Christ crucified . . . Christ the power of God and the wisdom of God" (1 Corinthians). In his later epistle to the Romans Paul said, "God had designated Jesus Son of God in power according to the spirit of holiness by his resurrection from the dead."[7]

In other words, for Paul, Jesus' divinity arose following his resurrection from the dead, after the fact you may call it. Now watch how the point of divination moves further back in Jesus' life as the Church moves forward in its development and apart from Judaism.

About fifteen years later the Gospel of Mark appears. Mark accepted, or confirmed, Paul's earlier declaration that God had designated Jesus to be God's son. However, for him this occurred not following the resurrection, but at the time of Jesus' baptism. Recall the voice of God spoke from heaven, Mark declared, and said of Jesus, "This is my beloved son in whom I am well pleased" (Mark 1:11). So with Mark, Jesus begins his ministry with the divine mantel at his baptism.

Next came the Gospel of Matthew, some decade or two later (now some 50 to 55 years following Jesus' life) and the proclamation of Jesus' divine origin moves again. It would appear that for Matthew it was an intolerable idea that Jesus became something either at his baptism or at his resurrection that he was not already. So, following Mark's logic that the resurrection simply revealed fully what God had proclaimed at this baptism, Matthew expands that to say both the baptism and the resurrection revealed only that which had been present from the moment of Jesus' conception. Hence from Matthew (and again later in Luke) we get the nativity story of the virgin birth. God still declared Jesus to be the Son in this gospel. But this time it wasn't God directly who provided the message. It was declared in a dream to Joseph by an angel bearing God's message of this good news.

The evangelist Luke, writing some five to ten years after Matthew's Gospel appeared, tweaked Matthew's details a bit and made his images more concrete and historical. But he essentially left the story line intact. Apparently for Luke, beginning Jesus' divinity from birth was about as far back as you could expect to take it. Luke, however, was wrong! He underestimated the ingenuity of the early Christian theological/philosophical mind.

By the turn of the year 100 or so, Jesus' identity/association with God had become so complete in the minds of his now mostly gentile followers that he was said to have somehow shared in that divine identity prior even to his conception and birth. It remained for the author of the fourth gospel, the Gospel of John, to formalize this understanding. The Gospel of John stands apart from the previous three gospels in that it is about Jesus as God, not as the earlier versions which were primarily about Jesus and God.

So, from the point of the resurrection at the end of his earthly life, back to his baptism at the beginning of his ministry, then back to his very birth; and now in John, back forever. The divine being of Jesus was for this latter evangelist the moment when the Logos, meaning the word of God, which had been part of God's very being since the dawn of creation, was born into the natural order. So, for John, there was no time in all human history when Jesus was not God's son.[8]

That's quite a theological progression, or maybe in this instance we should call it a regression. But it would take a few hundred more years before the Church declared orthodox the position that Jesus the Son, and God the Father were the same, i.e., of one substance. We'll get to that in a bit. Now let's return to the issue of salvation through Jesus Christ.

Recall we were talking about God's approach, or at least the Church's story line, to saving us poor sinners. That God in his love decided to transfer our collective guilt—past, present and future—on to (or in to) the person of the Son Jesus, and to sacrifice his incarnate self as payment (ransom) for our sins. Now you gotta admit that's quite a plan, Rube Goldbergish or not!

In this way, says the Church, the god of the idea has provided a clear path for mankind to approach, or reapproach itself, God, *without guilt*. It repairs, apparently, the purported falling-out between God and man that was the result of Adam and Eve's transgression in the Garden of Eden. Isn't that miraculous (and it only took this god about 2,500 years to get around to doing this)? Maybe, but some might consider this action as hinting that perhaps God made a bit of a mistake, or over-did his condemnation of Adam and Eve; he is trying to "make amends." To my way of thinking, that's a rather far-out but not an impossible stand to take. Still, I doubt if you (or I) could sell that to either adamant believers or the Church.

Another thought you might ponder is this: if the Book of Genesis is in its presentation largely myth and legend as modern biblical scholarship suggests, then it follows that the first biblical man, Adam, really wasn't (In the Greek Orthodox Christian Church Adam represents mankind, not a specific individual). If there really wasn't an original first man, how does original sin occur? I mean think about it, can we have a doctrine of original sin without an original sinner? Hmmm.[9]

Nonetheless, the belief that man has a sinful or "dark side" neither is nor was new during biblical times. Alan Jacobs in his super 2008 book about its cultural history, *Original Sin,* cites several instances of wrong-doing and the price that future generations of the wrong-doer paid for it. Greek artists and thinkers sometimes wondered whether the sheer prevalence of impiety and arrogance suggested something—something worrisome—about the very shape or form of humanity.

The last and longest of Plato's dialogues, the *Laws,* begins like a joke, says Jacobs: "a Cretan, a Spartan, and an Athenian are walking down the road" . . . At one point in the dialogue, the three companions discuss the crime of temple robbing. In the last few lines Kleinias, the Cretan, portentously affirms, "We must take the road along which God himself is so plainly guiding us." This crime strikes the Athenian as one that particularly needs explaining, and in explaining it he says something curious: the impulse to do such things "comes neither from man nor from God; tis an infatuate obsession that is bred in men by crime done long ago and never expiated, and so runs its fatal course." A few lines earlier he had spoken of "our universal human frailty," as though all human beings carry within them an inherited curse, a moral "frailty" that we derive from some evil ancestor.

Interestingly, this concept of the dark side of humanity is not exclusive to the West. Jacobs tells of an Oriental connection: The most famous of the Chinese sages, Kong Fuzi—better known to us as Confucius (551-479 BCE)—produced a disciple-sage some generations later named Xún Zi (310-237 BCE). "The nature of man is evil," he wrote. "Man's inborn nature is to seek for gain. If this tendency is followed, strife and rapacity result and deference and compliance disappear. By inborn nature one is envious and hates others."

Some might say people often, or at least sometimes, do virtuous deeds. So, if our nature is evil, where does goodness come from?

Xún Zi has a ready reply: "All propriety and righteousness are results of the activity of sages and not originally produced from man's nature . . . the sages gathered together their ideas and thoughts and became familiar with activity, facts, and principles and thus produced propriety and righteousness and instituted laws and systems."

So it would seem that the news from Xún Zi is not so bad after all. Yes, we have an innately evil nature and come into this world predisposed to greed and strife. However, these tendencies are correctable by the judicious enforcement of well-made laws. Xún Zi believes that "every man in the street possesses the facility to know humanity, righteousness, laws and correct principles and the capacity to practice them." His matter-of-factness is noteworthy and rather attractive. What his philosophy indicates is that one can have a very low view of human nature without being what William James calls a "sick soul": a person tormented by consciousness of sin and helpless in the face of temptation.[10]

Man's sin, whether innate or caused by an external event, is the subject of the Church. Without sin, what is the meaning of the Church's story of Jesus? That story is of salvation, and salvation from sin. Biblically it's the story of redemption from the sin of one man (and woman) that the Western Church insists all subsequent humanity is guilty of and must pay for—unless relieved of through the message of the Church's purpose of Jesus. That's a "got ya" message that's hard to ignore, or certainly has been in the history of the Christian Church in all its manifestations. Belief, says the Church, is your only "hope" of salvation; your only option for eternal life. Myself, I kinda like Xún Zi's conclusion. Yeah, we people inherently have our "dark side" but for the most part, and for most of us, it's controllable in our own best interests.

One might argue that Xún Zi's theory of sin is more applicable to a social or community understanding than to a theological one. One that rules and regulation can overcome, or at least keep in check. But on further thought about this, the Church is doing no more or less. It's just offering a longer term "potential" reward or penalty to motivate its audience. It lacks any consequential penalties for people acting in accordance with their dark side—aside from guilt—in the here and now which is where its version or representative of the god of the idea (Jesus) is perceived active in people's lives.

And finally on this specific subject, a historical glance at the evolving trend of the lay-public's perception of the significance of the dark side of human nature. It shows that what the Church chooses to emphasize, inherited-by-all sin, erasable by nothing less than complete faith in and dependence upon the Church may by many be considered "over-kill" as we move forward in time.

About the year 1049 an Irish monk (no less) composed a dream-vision narrative, the *Vision of Tondal*, which was widely read throughout the Middle Ages (as late as the fifteenth century). In his dream, Tondal is given an angel-guided tour of the afterlife, in which he sees various rewards and punishments. Among the groups he is shown is something like a place of mild punishment—suggestively a full-fledged Purgatory is on its way, though not yet arrived—whose inhabitants the angel describes. "These," the angel says, "are the wicked, but not very."[13] This might be said to be a lucid and brief summary of the then view of original sin that grew stronger and stronger throughout the sixteenth and seventeenth centuries, and on into the present.

We might quote this story to demonstrate a point: despite all the Reformation could do to emphasize our utter depravity and consequent absolute dependence on the grace of the Church's God, increasing numbers of people, while acknowledging the reality of our dark side, or original sin, if you wish, preferred to mitigate its consequences; yes, we are all the wicked, but not very![11] Today many might readily concur that there is a dark side of human nature, human self-interest, and characterize this threatening Church doctrine as a hangover from a less literate and questioning congregation; perhaps in many eyes, nothing more than a tempest in a tea pot. That puts the Church in a tough spot.

As I mentioned, in a very real sense the Western Church has taken the philosophy of Confucius' disciple-sage, Xún Zi, to heart in dealing with the dark side of humanity. Rather than "control it" by the governing by wise sages (philosopher kings) who recognize it and govern society to control and keep it in check, the Church employs the image of a wise sage (the Messiah) to do the same thing. They lift it from the shoulders of man by promoting the grace and/ or invoking the fear of the god of the idea, keying off the peoples' inherent concern of their own (inherited?) mortality. In this sense, one should give credit where credit is due, and I do believe some credit is due the Church in this connection. But as I mentioned, the Church is in a tough spot if people nowadays have a tendency to minimize the impact/consequences of what they consider a normal state of humanity-wide "sin" and question the solution the Church offers.

Just how does the Church respond to the argument that (a) we are all made in the image of God; (b) sin, or wickedness—but not very—is part of our human nature; (c) that must be how God intended us to be and act. If the Church's answer is, "Perhaps, but that must be how God has planned for your salvation through Jesus." One is led to retort, say what? Why? And the only answer I can come up with, as the Church, is "Well, it's a mystery."

It is not my intent here to sound disparaging, or to caricaturize the Church's arguments for the significance or meaning of Jesus. Rather it is to put them into contexts, then and now. These arguments, the Church's story, challenge rational understanding today. Especially so in the West, in a cultural environment very different from biblical and even post biblical times. Yet we are expected to accept them today, as in times past, because they continue to represent the Church's religious conviction. Again I reiterate, times have changed, but it seems the Church hasn't (conceptually or doctrinally can't; how do you change a long expressed truth without admitting error?). Truth we have said is not relative. However, if truth is as I have likewise expressed contingent upon context, perhaps you reexamine the context. The Reformation was certainly a challenge to the truth of the Church and led to significant change in the rise of Protestantism (more on this later).

But anyway, how is this sin-guilt supposedly lifted from the shoulders of mankind by Jesus? The "default" Christian supposition is that Christ's suffering made amends for human malfeasance. In what possible way? Through atonement; what is known today in the Church as substitutionary atonement.

Substitutionary atonement is the name given to a number of Christian models of the hypothesis that all regard Jesus as dying as a substitute for others instead of them (Jesus, through his death, did for us that which we can never do for ourselves). There are a number of differing theories that come under the umbrella term "substitutionary atonement." The four best known are the Early Church Fathers' ransom theory; Anselm of Canterbury's satisfaction theory, penal substitutional theory and a demystified version of the ransom theory called Christus Victor. I should mention that not all branches of Christianity adopt an atonement theory of the Cross, the Eastern Orthodox, for example.[12]

I'll limit my comments regarding atonement theories to the amazing penal substitution theory with which I and most Reformed Church goers (Protestants), certainly here in the USA, are confronted with come Sunday mornings. It's said to work as follows:

God is just. Justice, divine or human, requires that wrongdoers whose wrongdoing makes them liable to punishment should be punished. Humans, one and all, are sinners, i.e., wrongdoers. As such they incur a penalty which in justice ought to be paid and which according to the Church has, in fact, been paid. However, it has not been paid by those who owe it and deserve to pay it, but by Jesus. The verdict never changes: We-all-are-sinners. Sinners are guilty. But because he died, the sentence has been suspended for everyone else. Instead of punishing (God's wrath), God pardons (God's grace)! That's supposedly the gospel, the good news (My thanks to Charles Hefling, former editor-in-chief of the Anglican Theological Review for this summary explanation, writing in *The Christian Century*).[13]

That's an incredible hypothesis, if you stop to think about it, at least in this day and age. As an explanation of atonement it may be considered biblical in its basic origins (Romans 3:25; Hebrews 2:17), but Reformational in its present day understanding. Earlier atonement versions were a Ransom Atonement theory, and a Moral Atonement theory. It's at best a latter-day Reformed Church developed rationalization; a theoretical model. And we, who purport to be Christians, or at least have Christian leanings, are supposed to accept and believe it on faith alone. That's a bit hard for some, including me—I don't know about you—who rely heavily on reason backed up by pragmatic experience, not to mention common sense.

Penal substitution preaches well at the emotional and imaginative levels. Can't you picture Christ taking your place, enduring the pains you ought to have felt—because you-are-a-sinner, guilty of simply being, over which you had and have no control. Still, depending upon just how guilt-ridden you might be, how can you not be grateful for and bow down before this one assuming your mortal penalty; not *removing* your sin, but *paying* the consequences of it. Though that is the emotive power of penal substitution atonement, is that sufficient to accept its dependability; its truth? For many, the answer is undoubtedly, yes. But for a questioner, like me, and maybe you too, it's suspect (wishful thinking?). This atonement by penal substitution is attractive, and it sounds good—perhaps even plausible—but only until you really think about it.

Thinking about it, one rather traditional argument opposing atonement in terms of penal substitution makes rational sense to me: we conceive the god of the idea as just. His divine justice, better defined, is *retributive justice*, which attaches rewards to merit and penalties to fault. This is how God's justice is described throughout the Bible. As such, it's hard if not impossible to rationally (or otherwise) fit penal substitution inside this definition of justice. Consider: It's just to punish the guilty, but obviously, unjust to punish the innocent. Jesus Christ was proclaimed innocent, without sin (Hebrews. 4:15). If God used the acts of unjust men to bring about a divine plan that ended up punishing one guiltless and without sin, then God, in the end, is not just, no matter who (or what) Jesus was.

Recognizing this internal contradiction there are two possible rebuttals. Both questionably "hold water." The first introduces the remarkable claim that Jesus *was* guilty, but only because the guilt of others was transferred from them to him. How, for heaven's sake? How do you siphon the guilt from one human being into another, or from one generation to another? Can one will his guilt onto another, as well? In either case, accepting this response undermines if not eliminates the concept of moral responsibility. Think what that does to the concept of justice, divine, or otherwise.

The second, that punishing the innocent, though admittedly wrong, can in exceptional cases be just, provided it serves to "send a message," to dramatizes the heinousness of disobedience in order to deter those who might be inclined to disobey. Isn't that what today we generally refer to as terrorism? How just is that?

The point is these oft-used rebuttals to objections to atonement conceived in terms of penal substitution are themselves openly exposed to rationally shatter. Both rebuttals lend themselves to, as some put it, descriptions of atonement as divine child abuse or the vengeful violence of a tyrannical god. Retributive justice does leave something to be desired as an intelligible framework for making sense of the cross. For me, it is but yet another nail in the coffin of the Christian presentation of Jesus as the god of the idea. And the usual Church answer to my concerns is, "Well, we really don't know. It's a mystery."

Under the Western Christian conception of God ("Our Father who art in Heaven") that response is not just incredible, it's simply self-defeating. "It's a mystery," but we have to accept and believe it anyway. That seems always to be the fallback if no other justification or rationalization exists. In spite of all the knowledge and information we claim to have and know—how God works, how we can "serve" and please God, what God wants and doesn't want—about such a critical notion put forth by the Church, their answer is, we really don't know: "It's a mystery." Simple ignorance; end of story.

I note, however, that being "a mystery" is not necessarily the same as "the mysterious," or "mysticism," both of which have figured in the history of God through time and still significantly do today in the Eastern Churches. To my way of understanding, the atonement theory of penal substitution is neither mysterious or a mysticism. It's a supposition, a theory the Church simply can't defend in any other modern day fashion.

And this unsatisfying but understandable response leads me into another area that's a further doubt producer for me: unchanging truth confronting an increasingly enlightened, liberal, and progressive worldview. Where in all this is evidence, or even an indication, that Jesus was, or was at the time of his ministry considered, divine? He certainly did not so claim in any of his (probably authentic) sayings that have come down to us (Recall my earlier injunction that everyone is entitled to their own opinions, but not to their own facts). We have seen above how the Church manipulated, or at least reinterpreted, his proclaimed divinity. That he was special, as portrayed, seems beyond dispute. That some of his followers were convinced he had the blessings of God, and promoted such belief seems conclusive.

Throughout his whole brief preaching ministry Jesus emphasized the virtue of faith, or trust, and considered this to be a precondition for any valid action leading to the Kingdom of God. In the course of his whole public life-work Jesus behaved as a man (repeat, a man) conscious of being endowed with God-given power to perform charismatic deeds. He also demanded from his prospective "patients" total belief in his ability to cure them and it has been underlined again and again he went so far as to credit the faith of the sick person with the achievement of the actual healing (Mark 4:36; Matt 9:28; 17:20; Luke 18:42).[14]

As is often the case, the further away we get from the origins of a happening, the larger than life story it seems to become. Stories and fantasy become "facts." For the promotion of this we must look to the Church, as well as people's willingness, perhaps even need, to believe. The Church filled a need in people's lives, and Jesus filled a need, the justification for the Church to exist. In this sense we might say that Jesus filled a need in people, a need directed and fostered by the Church. And the Church moved on, divinely magnifying this martyr as it did so.

But in the process of moving on, differences in theological understandings and scriptural interpretations understandably came up. For hundreds of years, the Church was more horizontal in its hierarchy than its later vertical organization. Let's look for a moment at the brief history of one of the best-known controversies from the fourth century. Its impact is with us today. Two historical figures, Arias and Athanasius, stand out in this tumultuous fourth-century watershed about the divinity of Jesus.

It was not specifically about his "divinity," but rather about the divine position, nature, or status of Christ the Son/Logos, vis-à-vis God the Father. Now that Christianity had become a gentile faith, people found it difficult to understand Jewish terms, such as Son of God or Spirit. Was Jesus divine in the same way as the Father? And was the Holy Spirit another god? The debate focused on a discussion of Wisdom's song in Proverbs which began: "Yahweh created me when his purpose first unfolded, before the oldest of his works." (Proverbs 8:22-23) Did this mean that Christ was a mere creature, and if so, how could he be divine?

In a challenge to Alexander, bishop of Alexandria, which he found impossible to ignore but even more difficult to rebut, Arius, a charismatic presbyter (a lay church leader) in Alexandria, insisted that Jesus was a human being who had been promoted by God to divine status (this would tend to place God within time and history, contrary to our earlier understanding). He was able to produce an armory of scriptural texts to support his view. Arias argued that the very fact that Jesus had called God his 'Father' implied a distinction between them, since paternity involves prior existence; he also quoted gospel passages that stressed the humanity and vulnerability of Christ.

Athanasius, secretary (and later successor) to Alexander and in support of his bishop, took the opposite view: Jesus was divine in the same way as God the Father—an equally controversial idea at this time—which Athanasius backed up with his own proof texts (which it would seem keeps God out of time and history).

Allow me to paraphrase and condense how Geza Vermes, in his 2012 Book *Christian Beginnings,* presents this interesting bit of already mentioned religious history.[15]

As hard as it might be for us to imagine today, their disagreement triggered a seismic upheaval within the Church in Egypt. That soon spilled over to the entire Eastern Mediterranean. Recall that the Emperor Constantine had put an end to the persecution of the Church in 312. Bearing in mind the potential impact of the large body of Christians on the realization of his ultimate aim—civic peace in the empire—the emperor took an immediate interest in ecclesiastical matters. He was determined to intervene and settle the conflict in Egypt. Recall also at this point in Church history orthodoxy on much of Christology was still sort of by consensus. Let me explain.

Ever since the New Testament era and through the next two centuries equivocation about the divinity of Christ was standard, yet one point was certain: The Son was not recognized as having quite the same dignity and standing as God the Father; the same judgment applied *a priori* to the Holy Spirit. The pre-Nicene Church held a subordinationist view, asserting a degree of difference within the same sacred class in regard to the persons of the Trinity. The doctrinal stance adopted by the famous historian, theologian, and ecclesiastical politician Eusebius, bishop of Caesarea (c. 260-339), offers a characteristic example. Eusebius was unwilling to place Father and Son on an equal footing in the divine hierarchy. Relying on New Testament terminology borrowed from Paul and John, Eusebius agreed to grant the titles "Lord" and "God" to the Son or Logos/Word as long as it was recognized that the Son was ranked after and stood below the Father. Why was this?

It seemed the only escape route away from the trap of suspected formal Christian polytheism was by denying equal status to the various persons within the single Trinitarian Deity. Only the Father was fully *the* God; the Son was only the second or lower god, and the Holy Spirit something vague and unspecified, floating somewhere below the Son. Such a standpoint entailing gradation was the conviction prevailing prior to the outcome of the Council of Nicaea.

This general view, or *opinion communis*, held by all the leading lights in the Church for two and a half centuries and reinforced and expressed with unquestionable clarity by Arius and his allies, was challenged, attacked and finally overturned by a minority of bishop with the backing (and presence) of the emperor at the Council of Nicaea in 325.[16]

Allow me to add a paragraph from Karen Armstrong's 1993 best seller, *A History of God,* that kind of rounds out this story and gives it not only some context, but a touch of the common man in this brouhaha:

"In about 320 a fierce theological passion had seized the churches of Egypt, Syria and Asia- Minor. Sailors and travelers were singing versions of popular ditties that proclaimed that the Father alone was true God, inaccessible and unique, but that the Son was neither coeternal nor uncreated, since he received life and being from the Father. We hear of a bath attendant who harangued the bathers, insisting that the Son came from nothingness, of a money changer who, when asked for the exchange rate, prefaced his reply with a long disquisition on the distinction between the created order and the uncreated God, and a baker who informed his customer that the Father was greater than the Son. People were discussing these abstruse questions with the same enthusiasm as they discuss football today."[17]

Kind of makes one wonder if the tabloid press was geared up even way back then!

So, while there was a Church-wide consensus of the divine positions of the Father and the Son at the beginning of this controversy, there was no orthodox teaching on the nature of Christ and nobody knew whether Athanasius or Arius was right. Discussion [had] raged for over two hundred years. It was impossible to prove anything from scripture, since texts could be found to support either side—reminiscent of the issue of slavery in our Civil War. But the Greek fathers of the Church did not allow scripture to dominate their theology. In the creed he formulated after the Council of Nicaea, Athanasius used an entirely unscriptural term to describe Jesus' relationship with God: he was *"homoousian,"* of one substance, with the Father. Other Church fathers based their theology on religious experience rather than a detailed reading of the Bible, which could not tell us everything about a God who transcended all human words and concepts.[18]

Thus, eventually, it was less than the unanimous Church hierarchy that issued the edict that Jesus was (effectively) the god of the idea, some three-hundred years after his life; a position fulfilling to the Church and no doubt comforting for believers. That made it a win-win situation, true or false. Nonetheless there remained Christians after this announcement that continued to question it for some time. Eventually, "orthodoxy" won out. And remember, it's the victors who get to write history. Still, the end result with which we live today, the Son, the man Jesus, was declared consubstantial—of the same substance—with God the Father, by the Church, not unequivocally by the revealed word.

Skipping ahead to today, the Jesus of first century didactic presentation (the teaching of the twelve apostles) is questionably still the bedrock of Christianity. It is more the holy Jesus of the Gospel of John and the letters of Paul who we observe. In America, at least, Jesus is synonymous with the Western anthropomorphic god of the idea. But, in the eyes of those sitting in the pews, does their Jesus of today represent the same religious example as that early didactic presentation? I think it safe to say that in the view of the Church he does not—cannot after the canonization/deification he received from John, Paul and the Apostolic fathers of the second century and the decision made at Nicaea in 325. In some ways, the laity's view of the Church's Jesus must be confused, not what it once was. Once his position and meaning seemed all but unquestioned. Today with a more informed public and a more splintered Church it appears to be questioned, both what he is and what his meaning for Christians as well as for people at large may represent.[19]

Is he, can he really be, the god of the idea; and as such the savior for me personally and for mankind in general? Said differently, am I—and everyone else in the world– personally truly a sinner in need of salvation (deliverance from the power and penalty of sin) in the eyes of the Western god of the idea? On what basis? Sin, Original Sin? On the latter day biblical basis that the first purported persons committed a single act displeasing to their creator, some four or five thousand years ago and so everyone for all times must pay for their one transgression?

That seems to be what the Church, and especially the reformed (Protestant) Church has been preaching, and it is highly questionably attributable to the Bible aside from one single (repetitive) reference, Romans 5:12, where Paul says, "Therefore just as sin entered the world through one man, and death through sin, and in this way death came to all men because all sinned." This appears to be an expanded thought from his earlier penning in 1 Corinthians, 15:22-23 wherein he had written, "For as in Adam all die, so in Christ all will be made alive."[20]

This basic "whip" the Church holds over man merits some elaboration and clarification.

So, having already exposed a "dark side of human nature," just exactly what is the Church's "Original Sin?" Simply, the disobedience towards God, committed by the first of God's human creatures: the fable of the eating of the apple in the Garden of Eden. The concept of Original Sin was first alluded to in the second century by Irenaeus, Bishop of Lyons, in his controversy with certain dualist Gnostics. It was to the later Bishop of Hippo, St. Augustine (354-430), that the Christian Church in the West truly owes its legacy.

Augustine's theological contribution to the Western Church was, to say the least, very significant, particularly as an apologist/ defender for orthodox Christianity, especially against the heresy of Pelagianism. During his lifetime, were dark and terrible times in the Western world. The barbarian tribes were pouring into Europe and bringing down the Roman Empire; the collapse of civilization in the West inevitably affected Christian spirituality. Considering this situation, a deep sadness informed Augustine's latter works: the fall of Rome influenced his doctrine of Original Sin which would become central to the way Western people would view the world.

Based upon his reading of St. Paul, Augustine believed that God had condemned humanity to an eternal damnation, simply because of Adam's one transgression. The inherited guilt was passed on to all his descendants through the sexual act, which was polluted by what Augustine called "concupiscence." Concupiscence was the irrational desire to take pleasure in mere creatures instead of God; it was felt most acutely during the sexual act when our rationality is entirely swamped by passion and emotion; when God is utterly forgotten and creatures revel shamelessly in one another. This image of reason dragged down by the chaos of sensations and lawless passions was disturbingly similar to Rome, source of rationality, law and order in the West, brought low by the barbarous tribes. By implication, Augustine's harsh doctrine paints a terrible picture of an implacable God:

"Banished [from Paradise] following his sin, Adam bound his offspring also with the penalty of death and damnation, that offspring which by sinning he had corrupted in himself, as in a root: so that whatever progeny was born (through carnal concupiscence, by which a fitting retribution for his disobedience was bestowed upon him) from himself and his spouse—who was the cause of his sin and the companion of his damnation—would drag through the ages the burden of Original Sin, by which it would itself be dragged through manifold errors and sorrows, down to that final and never-ending torment with the rebel angels…So the matter stood; the damned lump of humanity was lying prostrate, no was wallowing in evil, it was falling headlong from one wickedness to another; and joined to the faction of the angels who had sinned, it was paying the most righteous penalty of its impious treason."[21]

Wow, that's heavy! One in recent times might be tempted to describe St. Augustine as the Reinhold Niebuhr of his own generation.

Biographically it needs to be said that this difficult heritage Augustine left us with is from a man who himself felt a great deal of self-guilt. A man who enjoyed the pleasures of the flesh prior to his conversion to Christianity, enjoying a long-term relationship with the mother of his child, neither of which appear to figure in his life following his conversion to Christianity and who has been quoted as saying, "Lord give me chastity…but not yet." He was a Platonist with a background in his younger years in Manicheism, a

Mesopotamian form of dualistic Gnostic cosmology between a good spiritual world of light and an evil materialist world of darkness. It flourished between the third and seventh centuries, briefly becoming the main rival to Christianity.

So there we have the background. What has been the eventual result of the promotion of "Augustine's doctrine" of Original Sin? Well, it is anything but universally accepted. Opposition to Augustine's ideas about Original Sin arose rapidly. After a long and bitter struggle the general principles of his teachings were confirmed within Western Christianity by several councils, especially the Second Council of Orange in 529, but have been interpreted in various ways since. Today, here is what we see:

JUDAISM:

Judaism regards the violation of any of the divine commandments to be a sin. Judaism teaches that sin is an act and not a state of being. Humankind was not created with an inclination to do evil, but has that inclination "from his youth." (Genesis 8:21)

EASTERN ORTHODOXY:

The Eastern Orthodox version of original sin is the view that sin originates with the Devil, "for the Devil sinneth from the beginning" (1st John 3:8). They acknowledge that the introduction of ancestral sin into the human race affected the subsequent environment for humanity. However, they never accepted Augustine's notion of original sin and hereditary guilt.

ROMAN CATHOLIC CHURCH:

By his sin, Adam as the first man, lost the original holiness and justice he had received from God, not only for himself but for all humans. Adam and Eve transmitted to their descendants human nature wounded by their own first sin and hence deprived of original holiness and justice, this deprivation is called "original sin." As a result of original sin, human nature is weakened in its powers, subject to ignorance, suffering and domination of death, and inclined to sin (this inclination is called "concupiscence").

THE REFORMED (PROTESTANT) CHURCH:

Martin Luther (1483-1546) asserted that humans inherit Adamic guilt and are in a state of sin from the moment of conception (In this he was certainly an Augustinian). In Lutheranism's Augsburg Confession is taught that since the fall of Adam all men who are born according to the course of nature are conceived and born in sin. That is all men are full of evil, lust and inclinations from their mothers' wombs and are unable by nature to have true fear of God and true faith in God.

John Calvin's (1509-1584) thoughts on mans' moral nature echo—and perhaps exceed—those of Luther. Calvin's view was one of man's total depravity, a doctrine, actually. In his *Institutes of the Christian Religion* he states, "Original sin, therefore, seems to be a hereditary depravity and corruption of our nature, defused into all parts of the soul, which first makes us liable to God's wrath..."

The various Protestant teachings about original sin seem, today, to be the most Augustinian around. There is little if any doubt in the minds of the various Protestant denominations here in the USA that we are, we really are, truly sinful and deprived beings who not only need but are totally dependent upon the grace of God—not only to make it through this mortal life, but to have any chance of anything but a future life of "hell." Still, even within the various denominations, one finds distinctions.

Bottom line here, I think you all get the official Church message here. Most of us are doomed from the get-go, but perhaps not quite all of us.

Go back and take a look at Martin Luther's Lutheran Augsburg Confession referenced above. It states all men who are born according to the course of nature are conceived and born in sin. "In the course of nature," I'm pretty sure, most would interpret as conceived as a result of sexual intercourse where St. Augustine's concupiscence occurs—and I have to agree with him, it or something very like it, does occur during this intimate person to person experience. But, what if, (like if there was no original man Adam, how could there be an original sin?), what if a human person is conceived and there is no sexual intercourse and hence no concupiscence involved? Yes, I'm thinking now of in vitro or artificial insemination to have children. This does not fit the Church's description of a sinful conception. Are they therefore born without sin? You know, I'm sure I'm not the first to think of this, and I bet further that the Church has an answer for it. A "yes, but" kind of answer. Still this issue fortifies my earlier observations regarding unchanging truth (or at least claims) in a changing world. It's a problem for the Church. But, back to original sin.

Even within the world-wide Church it's not a universal concept. But here in the West, it has gone pretty much unquestioned since the days of St. Augustine. At best, I suggest this concept is an example of *Peshar*, a form of biblical exegesis used by Jews and early Christians for their own ends.

If you really believe Augustine here, then it should be no problem believing that our biblical creator must have created man for nothing more than its own amusement; its own game of Chutes and Ladders, Monopoly or Pac-Man. Somehow such a scenario seems at odds with the historical trail of the idea of God we have followed here. How about the fallibility of our human nature, could that be the source of our "sin?" No, it would seem not. Fallibility is an inbuilt trait of humans, compared with God: God is perfect; man is imperfect. That's a given, and if as the Church-God made us and it was good, even if God subsequently decided to wipe out his creation and start over with one righteous family, we are what God created, assuming it was the god of the idea that indeed did create us as biblically presented. No, I think these historical justifications for our sinfulness seem increasingly unlikely to humanity today.

On what do I base this? The same visible falling away from the Church as highlighted above, especially here in the USA where Jesus is the title of choice for a personal God for so many. If fewer and fewer people are describing themselves as Christians and/or attending church, then it seems self-evident that the meaning or at least the significance of the personal Jesus, as presented, for them has waned. The Church's story must not be as convincing in today's world, as I have already suggested. Highlighting this in his recent book, *Church Refugees: Sociologists Reveal Why People are DONE with Church but Not Their Faith,* sociologist/author Josh Packard states there are 30 million "dones" in America—people who are finished with the Church but not ready to give up on their faith in God, or even their Christian identity.[22]

A major part of this is represented by the worldly progress man has made since biblical and post-biblical times, especially in the past five to six centuries. Part of this is a broadened approach to studying the Bible. Part of it I would attribute to the existence of a more educated, experienced and informed audience. Combine these elements, and if nothing more certain, doubt is created about the story, the belief in the Church and its implications for today. Doubt is created. Questions, whether verbalized or not, are asked. Unless and until the Church can address this doubt and these questions with something more than its traditional dogmatic, doctrinal and creedal responses, I suspect there will be more and more empty pews in church on Sundays. Surely people need (and want) something to believe in, but as we grow up we put toys away and recognize fairytales for what they are. Western man over the past 2,000 years has grown up, at least to some degree. I have little doubt that for as long as we can project, there will be a Christian Church. The issue is what it will represent, who it will serve, and what will be the consequences of it?

I asked above how did the simple Jewish Jesus morph into the god of the idea, the God Almighty of the Christian Church? The answer seems to be by evolution and historical circumstance and in the end, need or utility. It involves centuries long interpretation and philosophical development of the original historical story of Jesus producing differences in theological understanding and movements that challenged what was then considered common sense according to scripture itself—orthodoxy as yet undefined. We can't go into all of these here, but we can spend a few more paragraphs highlighting what, so far, has been the final outcome of this evolutionary—some might say revolutionary—process.

I believe most people are aware—if only from reading this—that what we today call Christianity at its inception was an exclusively Jewish movement. It developed within the Jewish faith. It was based upon the belief of a small sect that Jesus of Nazareth was, considering their direct personal experiences, the prophesized savior promised by the god of the Jews. This seems historically and biblically verifiable.

Christian development falls clearly into two unequal phases: the short Jewish opening period from CE 30 to about 100, followed by the Gentile expansion thereafter. The Synoptic Gospels—the biblical books of Matthew, Mark and Luke—and the first twelve chapters of the Acts of the Apostles, supplemented by the Judeo-Christian tractate the Didache, correspond to the essentially Jewish stage. In these presentations, the message preached by Jesus and his original disciples was addressed to Jewish circles in Galilee, Judea and Samaria.

However, in some of the New Testament writings one can already detect efforts by the Jewish authors to readjust the message to the requirements of a new Graeco-Roman pagan audience, the ultimate recipients of the apostolic teaching. Thus, a gloss inserted in the Gospel of Mark (7:19) cancels for all church members the Mosaic dietary rules. Also, the person ultimately responsible for the crucifixion, Pontius Pilate, is whitewashed in the story of the trial of Jesus, perhaps in order to render the gospel account less unpalatable to listeners or readers in the Roman Empire; many of such recipients were filled with hostility towards the rebellious Jews in the final quarter of the first century CE.[23]

At the beginning the message proclaimed by Jesus was a wholly theocentric one. That is, totally centered on God. Jesus played the role of the man of God, the leader, revealer, and teacher without being himself in any sense the object of worship. Jesus-worship came later in the fully-fledged Gentile Christianity inspired by Paul, and by the author of the Gospel of John, especially from the second century onwards. In the Synoptic Gospels, unlike the rest of the New Testament, the focal point of reflection and teaching is God, and not Jesus. It is towards God, the heavenly Father, that prayer and worship are directed without mediators (compare that with the Jesus oriented American Christianity). It is the Father himself who listens to supplications, offers a helping hand, and acts as protector, comforter and savior, surrounded by an aura of charisma. The religion practiced and preached by Jesus was meant to be a passport allowing the holder to enter directly the Kingdom of God. Christocentricity, it would seem, does not stem from the historical Jesus. Paul seems to have transformed the God-centered religion of Jesus into a Christ-centered Christianity.[24]

Christianity, as generally understood in the light of its Gentile development, and taking off in the late first century, is focused not on the genuine existential spiritual legacy of the Jewish Jesus. Its focus is on the intellectual acceptance of the Greek philosophically evolved divine Christ and his superhuman existence within the mystery of the Church's evolved triune Godhead.[25] While there was some scattered feeling that Jesus was divine, beginning as early as the second century, as we have seen, his coronation as God itself—one in the same—only took place during that Council of Nicaea (in 325) some three hundred years after his death. In some ways, this determination could be considered as much a political decision as a strictly theological one. The conclave, the first ever ecumenical council of Christianity, was convoked and financed by the Roman Emperor Constantine, who himself attended.

This long running difference of theological belief within the Eastern Church was brought to a head with that open disputation between Arias and his bishop, Alexander. This was dividing many and causing upheaval in the church, interfering with the Roman emperor Constantine's efforts to unite his empire in a peaceful manner.

Arias and his many followers believed Jesus divine, but inferior to God the Father. Alexander's position was he was co-equal with the Father. Technically Jesus was not declared "God" at the conclave (By this time most all Christians accepted Jesus, the Christ, as divine). By vote of the assemblage, the Son was declared of the same substance or essence *(ousia)* as the Father. In one word, he was *homoousious* or consubstantial with God. The practical theological result was that Jesus and the Father were "the same." Not one, necessarily, but the same.

For me that's not an easy description to either understand or describe. Nonetheless, it eventually became the official doctrine of the Church. While the council at Nicaea was primarily a Greek speaking event, the Latin (Roman) Church adapted it as well, even though its representation at the conclave was only about seven out of some 200 to 220 bishops attending. Some 1,800 were said to have been invited. What showed up is not what you might call the large expected turn-out. Even the Pope's two representatives failed to show up in person.

Nicaea ostensibly put an end to the orthodoxy of such subordinationist thinking. I say ostensibly because for at least the following fifty to sixty years such subordinate thinking persisted within the Church. The end came in 381 when Emperor Theodosius I made the profession of Arianism illegal. Thereafter consubstantiality carried the day and went on to feed the kind of philosophically based dogmatic evolution that was launched at Nicaea.

Since Nicaea the Christian religion has primarily been governed by intellectual and indeed philosophical assent, by adherence to the orthodox dogma of the Church.[25] By contrast, the piety preached and practiced by Jesus, consisting of a total surrender of the self to God and a constant search for God's Kingdom through limitless devotion and trust, was relegated to a supporting role in the Church. Charismatic Christianity was mostly kept away from the limelight, although occasionally it surfaced in a restricted form and not only in fringe movements but in various branches of Christian Pentecostalism.[26]

So at this point in the evolution of the Christian Church, both Eastern and Western branches, we worship the Lord Jesus as the god of the idea, because back in 325 some 220 mostly Eastern Christian bishops voted for the proposition (backed by the Roman Emperor) that Jesus and God the Father were of the same essence, or substance: consubstantiality. But even back then Christians were still confused. If there was only one God, how could Jesus also be divine?

Eventually three outstanding theologians of Cappadocia in Eastern Turkey came up with a solution that satisfied the Eastern Orthodox Church. Trained in Greek philosophy they were aware of a crucial distinction between the factual content of truth and its more elusive aspects (which today we might call fact vs. the mysterious, or the unknown, for lack of a better term). The early Greek rationalists had drawn attention to this. Plato had contrasted philosophy (which was expressed in terms of reason and was thus capable of proof) with the equally important teaching handed down by means of mythology (which eluded scientific demonstration). Later it was slightly modified linguistically by Augustine and found its home in the Western Church as well. That is, of course, the concept of the Trinity.

The Trinity—Father, Son, and Holy Ghost—is a book length topic of its own. So allow me simply to say, as developed and employed by the Church, it represents an insight in a Christian sense distinguishing between the public teaching of the Church based upon the scriptures—*kerygma*—and *dogma*, representing the deeper meaning of biblical truth which can only be apprehended through religious (mystic) experience and expressed in symbolic form. Translation: The Cappadocians were calling attention to the fact that not all religious truth was capable of being expressed and defined clearly and logically. Some religious insights, they held, had an inner resonance that could only be apprehended by each individual in his own time during what Plato had called *theoria*, contemplation. Besides their literal meaning, therefore, the scriptures also had a spiritual significance which it was not always possible to articulate.

This approach gave the Church a great advantage—only it could determine *dogma* (that was eventually challenged by the Reformation about a millennium later). As one of the Cappadocian Fathers expressed it, "These elusive religious realities could only be suggested in the symbolic gestures of the liturgy, or better still, by silence."[27] The Eastern Church clings today to this model. Here in the Protestant West we have become a much more talkative religion and concentrate on the public meaning of the scripture, the *kerygma*— *solo scriptura*—but still retain a Trinitarian God! Thus, the Greek and

Russian Orthodox Christians continue to find that the contemplation of the Trinity is an inspiring religious experience. For many Western Christians, however, the Trinity is simply baffling.[28]

I leave it at that.

Well, in considering the Jesus phenomenon here we have roamed a bit far and wide, but nonetheless, painted a picture or perhaps better said, traced an unfolding story based upon mostly historical fact and recent biblical/religious scholarship. We started off here with the question of Jesus' relationship to the god of the idea. We saw during the early Jewish years Jesus was considered a man, and by some the Messiah, especially favored by God. During formative years of the Gentile Church—post 100 CE for argument sake—there were varying opinions on just who and what Jesus was, what he represented. He was increasingly represented and promoted as more than a man. And it was the man Jesus that Gentile Christians were encouraged to pay homage to as being the incarnation of the god of the idea itself, come to earth to save mankind through the goodness of God Almighty. Admittedly, that's quite a story.

The Eastern Christian Church appears to have dominated the development of Christian theology during the early years, say until about the fifth century. As it matured the Church went through a number of schisms until eventually an orthodoxy was developed and put into place, to a large extent during the fourth and fifth centuries. While there have been adjustments and growing pains since then, a religious, or theological, status quo developed and held until about the early sixteenth century's appearance here in the West of the Protestant Reformation. In all of this, it is the figure of a highly Greek influenced presentation of the Semitic Jesus that at least Western Christians today are familiar with. Is that a proper and truthful presentation for the Church to offer its followers today?

Does Jesus = God?

In my humble personal opinion, the answer to this question is a qualified yes. Allow me to briefly justify this inconclusive conclusion, as we move on.

Chapter Eight

Does Jesus Equal God?

For me, and I still don't know about you, here's my lay perspective on that. Like most positions on the divine, you can neither prove it nor disprove it rationally. You either believe in it, or you don't. But in this case, with a historical record both as for the Church and for the man Jesus as we laid out in the last chapter, you can examine it and then reason about it.

The idea of God is instinctively real apparently because we—Western mankind as evolved socially and culturally, maybe even philosophically—need it to be. At least so far. I say again, it's a matter of utility; of the possibilities the idea offers us and the comfort it provides for us in the here and now. If you are a person of faith, it is supportive, even if a degree of skepticism or question is harbored. If you are a person lacking faith, it is still needed for you to dismiss.

The reality of the god of the idea, however, is more elusive; more difficult to substantiate on a rational basis, if you will. Proceeding from the reality of the idea to the reality of a "god-thing" of the idea is certainly not a given. The idea of God seems very wide-spread, but the adoption of the image of God itself is far from universal. In Christianity, the view of God between Western and Eastern Churches can differ significantly, as I have tried to show. But allow me to limit my comments to Christianity here in the West and more specifically to the United States.

Likewise, proceeding from the reality of the man Jesus—which seems historically verifiable—to the reality of Jesus as the god of the idea is rationally more elusive. Yes, there is the Bible. But that's all there is in this context. And keep in mind that the New Testament of the Bible is the product of Jewish and gentile Christian writers all. Their story begins with Jesus *and* God, and ends up being Jesus *as* God.

What the New Testament attests to for Jesus is the basis for the religion of Christianity. Jesus' eschatological preaching and later claims for salvation based upon a belief by some of a physical resurrection from death provided a compelling story, first to a segment of Jews and later to a much larger population of gentiles.

The Gentile Church is built around their story of Jesus based on a reworking and reinterpretation of the Jewish scriptures, the Hebrew Bible. The idea of God was around a long time prior to this. Pretty early on, as we have seen, the Church ruled that the Jewish Jesus and God the Father are, in effect, the same or at least equal. This was a radical shift at the time. They (which to me means more than one) are "homoousios," in the Greek; meaning of one, or the same substance. Once accepted as doctrine, this is the Church's story to disseminate, and obviously, defend. They have been doing so for a long time, such that most Western laypersons accept as "truth" the Church's teaching that Jesus equals God equals Jesus. Jesus and his early Jewish followers never claimed he was a god, or God the Father. What his followers did claim was that Jesus was the Jewish Messiah. He was touted as being the promised and expected deliver of the Jewish people, based upon their scriptures. You will recall that the Jews had been under foreign domination and influence for what must have seemed to them forever.

The nascent Church capitalized on this messiah concept and broadened its use of the term such to make it a divinity, not just a deliverer. Jesus the Jewish Messiah became Jesus the Christ (messiah in Greek), a gentile divine savior, with proclaimed powers of such. This understanding was subsequently raised to the equivalent of God Almighty, as we have seen here. Not necessarily that the Father and the Son are one and the same (we still have the Father <u>and</u>

the Son), just that they are the same, substance wise. It seems to be an important religious technicality that is difficult for some to understand, let alone grasp. It's just accepted.

And here is something else that is accepted. The Incarnation holds that in Jesus God assumed a human body. It affirms that Jesus was God-Man; simultaneously both fully God and fully man. That's the Church's Creed. It may seem paradoxical, even a blatant contradiction, but the Church had what it believed good and sufficient reasons for holding this position.

If the doctrine held that Jesus was half human and half divine, or that he was divine in certain respects while being human in others, our minds might not balk. But such concessions are precisely what the Creeds refuse to grant. In the words of the Creed of Chalcedon, Jesus Christ was "at once complete in Godhead and complete in manhood, truly god and truly man. . . of one essence with the Father as regards his Godhead, and at the same time of one essence with us as regards his manhood, in all respects like us, apart from sin."

It was apparently perceived "evidence" that forced the early Christians to their logic-taxing assertion that Jesus was both human and divine. Recall that these declarations, these Creeds and doctrines of divinity, took place about four hundred years after his death. The "evidence" we are speaking of represented religious experience over hundreds of years now—intuitions of the soul concerning ultimate issues of existence. Such evidence cannot be presented with an obviousness that will compel assent, for it does not turn on empirical evidence. But if we try we can arrive at at least an intimation of the experiential leads that the Church was following.

The two councils of Nicaea in 325 and of Chalcedon in 451 while officially deifying the man Jesus, in addition really redefined the idea of God itself, robing Jesus in divine terms and, especially the latter, God, in more emotionally human terms. The result was a symbiosis (joining) of the two ideas. The Incarnation claimed that there was something newsworthy in the Christian message; namely, its proclamation of the kind of God that God was, as demonstrated by God's willingness to assume a human life in the form that Jesus exemplified. That willingness, together with the character of Jesus' life, added up to a different understanding of divinity than the Mediterranean world had known. In the church's view, God was concerned about humanity; concerned enough to suffer in its behalf. This was unique, unheard of.

And faith and belief in Jesus was now faith and belief in the Christian God; the God who cared about humanity, about you. That's the good news. And it was all possible in Jesus Christ, mankind's bridge to the infinite. A bridge must touch both banks, and Jesus following these councils was religiously the bridge that joined humanity to God; the seen with the unseen. To have held that Jesus was man but not God would have been to deny that his life was fully normative and to concede that other ways might be as good. To have said he was God but not man would have been to deny that his example was fully relevant.[1]

Though the Christian announcement of the Incarnation—a God-man—was likely as startling to its day as it is to ours, the shock attaches to different poles. Because we find disturbing the thought that a human being can be divine, we find the shocking feature of the Incarnation to be what it says about Jesus, that he was God. But in his own world, where the dividing line between the human and the divine was perforated to the point that even emperors routinely claimed to be divine, a struggling sect's claim that its founder was divine likely raised few eyebrows. What else is new? would have been the common retort. Such is certainly less the case today.

For the times, the church's arguments here must have seemed as good as or probably better than what alternatives, religiously speaking, were available. Given a bit of time, they did eventually take hold, become orthodox, and we observe them to this day. It's hard to argue with success.

Therewith stands my answer to the above-qualified "yes". In effect they are the "same" for Christians because the Church says they are. For believers, it's a matter of faith in the Church. It's a dogmatic but at the same time highly utilitarian (useful) religious model. After some scrutiny, I would not care to have to defend it too rigorously today, as the Church must. Again the question, when does doubt creep in?

As an aside here, one comparison regarding the Trinity from way, way back then was, "see here: I have two copper coins. They are made of the same 'substance' (copper). Are they the same?" Well, they are separate (two) coins, but yes, they are the same. They are interchangeable, one can be used for exactly the same purpose as the other. I don't know if that example supports the Church's position or not, but it is descriptive of being of the same substance; they are in that narrow definition the same, or equal in purpose and value. But what if they were not produced or made at the same time? What if one anti-dates the other? Does that make them different, or one superior to the other? Beats me. And it almost seems beside the point.

And there is always the comparison of water, steam and ice: three natural or formable states of one basic substance we call water, itself a compound of two elements. There are no doubt other material examples of threes-in-one that might be used in support of the concept of a divine trinity. I do not myself believe they contribute very much to the argument, or issue, but people have used these as examples of the possible. You decide.

One issue here we can't avoid in considering Jesus' relation to God is just how you define the god of the idea. In the Western tradition, based upon the purported sayings of Jesus, the Church presents the god of the idea as "our Heavenly Father" or "our Father who art in Heaven," or even as the God of the Hebrew Bible is depicted (Genesis tells us we are made in the image of God). Therein God walks and talks with humans and already has ["his"] kingdom in Heaven. This implicitly depicts an image of this god in a superhuman ontological form somewhat relatable to humanity, i.e., anthropomorphically in the eyes of most. Going from a solo "Father" to a duo "Father and Son" divine relationship in such an understanding is not such a leap of faith that it might otherwise be.

For example, if the Western Church presented or defines God for its adherents in its more philosophical manner (the Godhead), such a leap of faith might be more difficult to make. There is an ancient metaphysical doctrine that the source of all things—God, that is—must be essentially simple. That is, God cannot possess distinct parts, or even distinct properties, and in itself does not allow even of a distinction between essence and existence. The simplicity at issue here is not physical but metaphysical. The principle of divine simplicity carries with it certain inevitable implications.

One is that God is eternal, not in the sense of possessing limitless duration but in the sense of transcending time altogether. Time is the measure of finitude, of change, of the passage from potentiality to actuality. Another implication is that God is in some sense impassible: that is, being beyond change, it also cannot be affected, or to be more precise, modified, by anything outside itself.[2]

It would seem difficult if not impossible to relate Jesus, a contingent being located within time and place, to a proclaimed absolute being, or self-contained power for which time and place are not only insignificant but meaningless. It may be possible to argue that such a God might extend Jesus certain characteristics or powers for finite purposes, but to maintain that the two are "of one essence" consubstantial, seems an impossible position to defend under the descriptions of the god of the idea as presented here. Furthermore, if being impassible, or "beyond change" is an apt description of the god of the idea then how can the Church change this by simple human decree as they did at Nicaea? Of course, one can always argue for a different presentation of the god of the idea that better fits the Western Church's teachings.

Back to Jesus and the question at hand.

Jesus, presented as the incarnation of God, is multi-culturally important. As with the god of the idea of God, whether he was/is or not is almost, as I say, beside the point today. That is how he has been presented, what he represents in Christianity and that is how many in the West relate to the god of the idea, in/as Jesus. The good is that it allows people to grasp the idea of God in a positive, personal and recognizable form, again, right or wrong. That has been important for keeping the idea of God culturally relevant.

The bad, if there is a bad, is what Western Christians may be unwittingly doing. They may be being idolatrous. That is, at the insistence of the Church, transforming something that is for mankind unknown and given our imperfect natures probably unknowable, into a symbol of that unknown god for purposes of obtaining the blessings of the idea itself. I can support that. It's very utilitarian and especially for the majority who take their faith seriously but do not question their religion in a similar fashion.

Were I debating the above position with the late existential philosopher and atheist, Sir Bertrand Russell, he would argue that my moral point of utility was insufficient to make this decision. His point (writing in 1930) was there is a certain tendency in our practical age to consider that it does not much matter whether religious teaching is true or not, since the important question is whether it is useful. He would insist that one question cannot be decided without the other.[3] Truth and open debate about learning was a central point with him. He was and is not wrong, in my opinion. But my vision of the world we live in, and the dictates we should follow for our maximum human benefit are perhaps not as black or white, or as logical, as he believed them to be.

Even if the good may not always be philosophically reconcilable with the true, that does not, ipso facto, make the good bad. Maybe that makes me a relativist after all. I take his point; it's valid, but it is too inflexible and ridged for me as I view the world around us. As I mentioned somewhere way back, I have no problem with lying to someone—right or wrong—if it's for their benefit (good), comfort, or peace of mind and causes no one any harm or ill effects. That's how strongly I believe in the usefulness of the concept of utility.

So, yes, while under today's conditions I may be skeptical of the presentation of the Church's god of the idea, I accept the role that Jesus has been assigned, for the comfort of we poor sinners—but not very—in the here and now. At the very best, their intentions in this regard are laudable.

What we think we know about the god of the idea we derive primarily from family influence and religious institutional instruction. This differs significantly depending upon your particular family and their and your Christian affiliations, although here in the West it generally supports the position that Jesus equals God. As I say, this may afford a convenient and comforting anthropomorphic vision of a God few could otherwise relate to and/or try to approach.

The identification seems of dubious validity, once one looks closely at the historical record from today's perspective, or vantage. Again, anyone is entitled to their own opinions, but not their own set of facts. Truth, while not relative, is we said conditioned by context. It is questionable, in my mind, if the Church really knows any more about the god of the idea than the man in the street does. What it does know more about is simply the Church's internally developed teachings. Today these seem more like teachings about their Christ than about our god of the idea, which in their minds seems inseparable. Okay.

Does that mean I'm anti-religious? No. Simply doubtful. I'm just not fully convinced of their theological story and its presentation. Here I think I could side with the Positivists: As we can in all probability never know the essence or substance of God—assuming God—the argument or question is probably meaningless from a rational point of view. Amen.

Chapter Nine

Picking a Path: The Church's Continuing Role Providing For Man's Non-Material Needs

To find a solution, you must identify the problem

The previous chapter could have been a good place to wind-down this (layman's) polemic. Chapters Five and Six summed up my understanding of the "what" and "why" of the idea of God. Chapters Seven and Eight summarized the same for the Church's understanding and development of its highly successful approach of bringing the idea of God to humanity in a manner that both provided for Western man's non-material needs (hope) and allowed him to have a here-and-now affinity with the god of the idea. And recall, it also influenced the perception of the then god(s) as never before in the Mediterranean region out of which it grew. Giving credit where credit is certainly due, over a two thousand year history that's pretty spectacular!

But that was then; what about now? Along the way here we have pointed out what appear to be growing stresses in the Church's relationship with modernity. The Church finds itself on the wrong side of history. Since at least the mid-twentieth century the global trends politically, socially and culturally have been to try and minimize authoritarian power and maximize cooperative or tolerant power arrangements nationally and internationally. By implication, this has affected individual understanding of individual and human rights – which have been enhanced by these cultural, social, and political tides. But one cumulative effect of change is it disrupts tradition. The Church represents authoritarian tradition. Therefore while in the midst of the liberalizing sea-change that has been going on throughout the West for decades now, it continues to resist even the idea of change that its adherents accept and adjust to as if, nothing else, the inevitability of life going on.

For centuries people believed and behaved morally as the Church directed under the threat of consequences. Even the civic environment was largely guided by religion. Truth, teachings, and obedience under threat of divine review was a widely accepted Church promoted basis for behaving – even for thinking. That's authoritarian.

R.R. Reno, editor of the conservative periodical *First Things* recently wrote, "We are living in a strange historical moment. The culture of the twenty-first century West lives at a greater remove from the perennial human desire to obey divine authority – a far greater remove – than any culture in human history." Mr. Reno describes our public culture as one of limited horizons and a pessimism that finds countless reasons why nothing new or bold can be done. "Sustainability" is our default aspiration. In a world without divine authority, tomorrow can only be a recycled version of today.[1]

I certainly can't argue with Mr. Reno. I would only ask about the causation producing this condition. Mr. Reno implies it lies at the feet of culture change. But for well over a millennium the Church, broadly speaking, was highly influential in cultural norms and their formation. What has brought about this apparent (sudden?) fall from religious cultural influence? That, I believe, is a question that merits looking into at this juncture. It's one consistent with man's need for non-material support in life. If not from the Church, from where, as we move ahead through history?

Its story seems for many today, and increasingly so say the poll numbers, not as compelling, perhaps not as credible as it was in times now mostly past. Having come this far in my theological chronical, it seems awkward, perhaps even cowardly of me, to side-step some speculation what the future might hold for the Church. That future, I should add, will undoubtedly affect us all, directly or indirectly, to some degree.

This best starts with an understanding about the past and the present, looking towards the future: the Church has a fixed historical internal vision of the god of the idea; of, it would claim, "truth." The Western world of the twenty-first century, contextually and otherwise, is not the same in almost any aspect as it was when this vision was developed some seventeen to eighteen centuries ago. But the Church in its approach to representing the god of the idea seems to be the same in most aspects.

Looking back and reviewing the present is the easy part. Looking ahead to what the future may bring is a bit trickier (and in all honesty, I didn't start out here with this in mind! However . . .). Tea leaves probably won't help much. You have to wonder just what the "present," religiously speaking, will look like one hundred years from now considering (1) what we have seen happen in the past few hundred years and (2) from present conditions and apparent trends. We have both external as well as internal factors to consider; the religious doesn't happen in a vacuum.

I guess I should start here with one rather obvious specific and then add a few broad general assumptions. The specific is that as we move forward mankind does not effectively destroy itself by some inadvertent or stupid actions. I sometimes wonder just what odds the bookies in Las Vegas would give on this. For devout believers, this is probably not a concern, given God's covenant following the Flood.[2] For the others:

First of my assumptions, given the above, is that progress as we have defined it as improvement in the human condition will continue. As in the past few hundred years, it may well be spotty, and unevenly distributed, but generally I believe you can expect to see your grandchildren's grandchildren better off overall than is the case today. This applies across race and ethnic lines. Opportunities for better and more wide-spread education will be available; healthcare will continue to improve; economically, individual achievement and personal financial security will be available. For those who are less able, or maybe even less inclined, they will find greater (if different) opportunity, with dignity, via State support (economically and socially), than they do in this day and age. Highly regulated capitalism will continue to be the market model for most, but it will be a capitalism that has learned (probably the hard way) that an increased social/community responsibility is both in its interest and will be required of it via government sponsored but largely business supported efforts. This will be but an extension of trends we see currently. Government (the state) is going to be an even larger factor in the lives of most.

The above are nearly all materialistic in nature, worldly in other words.

Second, consistent with the above cultural comments, politically a generally liberal attitude will prevail. Here in the US we will continue to be ideologically divided, but at some point in this process a so-called "Third Way" is liable to gain political ascendancy. This could occur exactly because a plurality of voters tires of the excesses of ideological politics hamstringing governing that is combative and high cost but of limited effectiveness for too many. What we have today is government that governs for most of the people only some of the time. This Third Way will attempt to govern for all of the people, at least most of the time. It will be democratic electorally, but somewhat autocratic internally so as to be disciplined in its promises to voters of serving all of the people at least most of the time. To accomplish this, it will need to govern from above, and less as the state is today, trying to govern from within, or micro-manage the country. This in itself will be no easy or unchallenged effort.

One might reasonably characterize the presidential election campaign of last year as widely pent-up frustration for this desire for change within the governing status quo. Unfortunately, the alternatives we have been offered by our primary election system seem all but to eliminate the expectation of any real positive outcome in this direction, irrespective of the final result. Pity. Opportunity wasted (I shall now descend from this soapbox!).

Third, urbanization/suburbanization will continue to be the preferred way of life, if for no other reasons than that's where housing and utilities are, schools and work can be found and civic/public security services are provided. Older developments within this demographic will be recycled. Nothing much new here.

Fourth, the trend toward economic and political globalization will continue and increasingly benefit almost everyone, everywhere. Such, I should mention, is not that apparent or obvious to everyone everywhere today. Regional and/or local inequality and loss of economic opportunity resulting in social stress needs to be addressed and off-set; and it can best (only?) be done by government. I believe it can be done to the satisfaction of all involved, and at an acceptable price, and, finally, without undue control or burden upon capitalism, or economies, be they developed or undeveloped. I can offer specifics in this area to those interested (am I still on the soapbox?). Migration will continue to be an option, but with improving local opportunity (progress) around the world, it will abate.

One cannot help but question some (or all) of these assumptions. There could be a lot of "ifs" in them. But we can't look very far ahead if we don't make some projections; these seem realistic and reasonable from what we know today. So with these, what are we looking at a hundred years from now, religiously? These are some of the significant "external" factors developing around the world, or in our case the country, within which the religious must exist.

Given the above, I don't see any obvious external threats to Christianity on the far horizon, although the possibility of Islam and Christianity continuing to be competitors seems a given. Closer to home I foresee an increase in ecumenical activities within the existing religious communities. For one reason: self-interest. Such activity may well lead to what we call in business consolidation for the common good (meaning continued existence, or survival) of all. It may seem far-fetched now, but give it fifty or sixty years. Here's why:

What we still experience today is a plethora of churches in town (or city). Many of them are marginal insofar as being self-sustaining. Yet many of them are so close to their competitors, belief-wise, practice-wise and other-wise that it only makes sense to consider consolidating to stay alive. Some people already do a lot of church hopping both within and between denominations. You may not see this happening next year, or the year after, but I do believe it is inevitable; call it a trend that certainly appears irreversible. As one writer has stated it, "As late as 1965 the mainline Protestant churches' members accounted for over half of all Americans, but after running out of money and members and meaning for decades they represent only about a tenth today. [3] That's a trend, folks. Need further evidence here, just consider all those church closings we spoke of earlier. How far will this go? Who knows, but I doubt if we will end up with just one Protestant and one Catholic congregation in a hundred years (well, maybe just one Catholic one). As far-out as this may sound today, time will tell.

The greater potential threat to the Church's fortunes I and others foresee, is an internal one, as I have already suggested. However, in fairness, it needs to be pointed out that this potential internal threat is not necessarily totally of the Church's own making. Still, while organized religion's vision of itself is that it gives unity to a genuine social aspiration of humanity is no doubt genuine, it seems increasingly irrelevant due to the changing shape or character of secular liberalism. The "changing shape of secular—and even sectarian—liberalism" is, in a nutshell, the church's main problem. I have characterized this repeatedly as "progress", agree with me or not.

In this sense, I would offer that the Church needs to more clearly understand—or perhaps better said, accept—the cause and extent of its predicament. While it is beyond the scope of our analysis here, it's probably necessary to go back to the outcome of the Protestant (and Catholic) Reformations of the sixteenth and seventeenth centuries to find the origins of this situation. But as a result of this epoch, I think the following observations are valid, and certainly form a part of the Church's internal views of itself today to be considered, vis-a-vis the world around it.

Catholicism continues to exhibit ecclesiology (Church doctrine) that is triumphalist, dialectical and militant; insisting that there is no salvation outside its walls (possibly softening, potentially, by the efforts of Vatican II). Responding to the anti-clerical political movements of nineteenth-century Europe, the Catholic Church maintained that it [alone] is a perfect political society, one that governs itself in sovereign independence of the state, showing humanity the true form of social unity and solidarity. While perhaps delivered in a more inclusive and positive sounding apologetics today, this pretty much still seems to be the internal, almost divine, view of itself.[4] I'm not saying, necessarily, that their view(s) are wrong, simply that today they are pretty counter-cultural in most Western developed societies.

Following its painful birthing throughout the sixteenth and seventeenth centuries, Protestantism became what we might call "straight-laced." That is, it prioritized above all else the faithful observance and discipline of the written Word of God, the Bible. It focused exclusively on the personage of Jesus, preaching and imposing religious and moral discipline on a reluctant populace, developing in the process what are referred to as "hard edges". Sin in Protestant thinking became the over-arching justification for its approach to theology. These were prioritized over then traditional Church teaching and discipline while splintering into seemly never ending schisms. Eamon Duffy, a professor emeritus of the history of Christianity, has described the Reformation(s) as the end of the moral and religious coherence of Christendom and the beginning of Christianity as we experience it today.[5]

While both Protestantism and Catholicism were going their own narrow—some might say closed-minded—spiritually preservative traditional ways, Western culture and societies were heading in an almost opposite liberal direction. Newer, or at least non-mainstream, religious alternatives became available. And so it continues today.

We are seeing the cumulative—and apparently continuing—consequences for these separate roads being traveled by the Church and the wider society. The church's ability to influence, "shape" or manage society apparently peaked with the Reformation. Since then, mainstream Christian religion has been swimming against the tide. Hence, their resultant "cultural" issues.

Both Church-factions continue to profess their societal significance as they simultaneously "circle their wagons" against the savage infidels (who are mostly their neighbors), while inviting into their circle any who can come to accept and believe on their own terms. That's fine. Some obviously can and do. But the picture presented here earlier is one of a significant and continuing loss of adherents. The problem thus becomes one of reconciling religion's insistent views of itself, its metaphysical self-understanding and spiritual objectives, with those of the broader society. Or, do they simply allow the gulf to get larger, and themselves less relevant? Big issue! And I mean this for both sides.

Parenthetically, for those interested in pursuing this Church/cultural issue, I can suggest two relatively recent books that consider it broadly, if not exhaustively. Sociologist Josh Packard's 2015 *Church Refugees* focuses on the so-called "Dones" with church—with a small "c"—and the Barna Group's David Kinnaman's 2007 book *Un-Christian, What a New Generation really thinks About Christianity ... And Why It Matters.* Both are critical research summations aimed, I interpret, at helping assist the Church to see the forest for the trees.

Back to business. As I pointed out, to the degree theology deals with important human problems, maybe the Church doesn't have to change that much. Maybe the Church simply has to recognize, even if this means up-dating the script, what those religiously important human problems are.

So the Church's internal problem seems one of reconciling longstanding historical purported religious truths and practices it espouses with equally or more persuasive modern day secular teaching and cultural change. Early Christianity's message, creeds, and dogma were all developed within a context of those times, and as such, were credible within those times. Most would agree the times have changed. It does not seem unreasonable or irreligious to suggest the original context no longer serves a present day cultural understanding, and should perhaps be reconsidered in order to keep its basic message credible. Call it the challenge between the conservative and the liberal to progressive views of religion. This is going to be wrenching for the mainline churches. As above mentioned, when religious ideas cease to be effective, they fade away. I would go so far as to say that the idea of God, or here in America, the idea of Jesus as a personal Savior-God, seems to be becoming an increasingly questioned issue. Is it becoming less effective as motivation for believing, along traditional lines? Some have already found alternate religious institutions to satisfy them, both more fundamental and more progressive in religious pursuit. At its extreme, we could be talking schism within the Church here. And aside from an expression of frustration in the popular vernacular, what does "Oh for Christ's sake" mean today?

Respect for the idea of God, and for the idea of Jesus as God, as presented by the Church, is certainly wide-spread and continues today in high repute, in my opinion. But also in my opinion, I see it being considered less and less personally necessary over time for an increasing portion of the public. Why should this be so? Like Mr. Reno, I lay it primarily at the feet of cultural change based in large part upon "progress," resulting in the individuals' perceived (personal) need for the idea of God; cultural change the Church is apparently less able to influence.

In my view, it's an extension of the rational individualism of the seventeenth and eighteenth century Enlightenment. God is good, even great, goes the thinking. But God is great primarily in an impersonal sense, less and less in an individual personal sense. Another possible cause is the thinking advanced by the Protestant Reformation: every man his own preacher; a declining feeling of need for or dependence on institutional religious intercession.

Some see as another reason for the decline in mainline Protestantism being the embrace and promotion of the social gospel, to a shift in the here and now religious emphasis that began early in the twentieth century. To some degree, we discussed this in Chapter Four.

Recall the three human longings, or needs, the idea originally and over time was seen to fulfill: protection, perfection and perpetuity. These three "must haves" are not all as powerful and beyond mankind's perceived reach as in eons now past, must go the thinking. "Progress" has lessened the perceived external or divine need for, certainly, protection. We are better able to comprehend and protect ourselves—individually and collectively—from the dangers and threats of the natural world.

As for perfection, that still seems well out of reach of just about all of us, as we define it (God like). But generally, progress is also bringing us within striking distance of that kinder, gentler world— relatively speaking. And we can see further avenues in how we should, and in many cases, try to do better in dealing with and providing for others. So while the idea of God (the good) certainly continues to move us in this direction, increasingly many seem to believe we are better able today to see the path ahead of us in this quest, absent the absolute need for the Divine to lead us individually by the hand any longer in these ethical and moral issues. But that general idea of God continues to provide us with an absolute good in setting ethical and moral standards.

Does that mean we don't need a church environment to encourage these strivings? I didn't say that. Remember, absent an idea of perfection, without an absolute (the good) to aspire to, morals and ethics become simply a matter of taste; no reason hate is worse than love, or war is worse than peace. Religion is essentially an inner feeling that there *is* a God.[6] Obviously, a church environment promotes such an inner feeling, or at least it should.

As for perpetuity, I'm at a loss what to say. People either believe in an afterlife, or they don't. Or, as is often the case, they don't really know but know what to hope for (á la Blaise Pascal)! I'm not sure believing in God is equivalent to believing in the hereafter, or vice-versa, but it's probably a good motivator even today. Some would respond that if there is a hereafter for individuals following human dying, God (as we presently understand it) probably has about as much to do with it as so many now believe God had to do with the biblical depicted creation of the world or appearance of man: probably not all that much.

As I personally have questions about "heaven" as depicted, I tend to see the presentation of an afterlife as a comfort to and for those in the here and now; to minimize the human anxiety of death, of personal extinction, as it draws near. Nothing I can see wrong with that. But then as I mentioned, I don't see sin in telling someone a lie, if it is for their benefit and/or in being kind and non-injurious to them. I believe the Church has played and can continue to play a positive role here.

So, if what has served as the purpose and effective attraction of the idea of God appears to be decreasingly meaningful, or personally necessary for many people today, the Church is going to have to come up with new reasons or motivations to observe the idea (the why of God), or it will in time simply fade away—as far-fetched as that might sound at this moment. And we have spoken some of this need. There is little doubt churches are aware of the problem, even if most might not articulate it in quite these terms. Most still appear to act as if they are certainly not out of step. After all, they rationalize, they have "the truth." They are offering access to it; for them there is nothing wrong with their message. They just need, they believe, ways to get more (and younger) people into church on Sunday mornings to listen to it (and hear it) in a more contemporary fashion. Maybe that will work. I doubt it.

The biggest visible shift I can highlight by the Church seems to be their increased emphasis on service, or in church-talk, mission. It may just be my imagination, but the emphasis of the idea of God seems to be shifting to less of protection and perpetuity and more to perfection. Not in the hereafter, but in the here and now. There is a movement, visible and seemingly growing if still small within the Western Church, which proposes the future for Christianity is to ameliorate the traditional conservative institutional practice of Christianity into what they would describe as a more "Christian" approach. They hold that any faith community that excludes, divides, judges or is intolerant is doing so outside of the model given to us by Jesus. They also accept that there are other paths that also lead people to an experience of God (Reminiscent of the late Catholic Father Jacques Dupuis's thinking that got him into trouble with Catholicism's C.D.F highlighted in Chapter Five).

It's a Protestant movement called Progressive Christianity. It asks the question, "What is the proper object of our worship?" Their answer seems to be Jesus as teacher, not exclusively as a divine Savior relating to sin and individual salvation, although it accepts Jesus as Christ, Savior, and Lord. Their rationale seems to be that adoration of the post-Easter Christ so dominates the language and liturgy of the church that the wisdom of pre-Easter Jesus is all but lost; that the divine Savior image is now so exclusively the message of evangelical and fundamentalist Christians that the Sermon on the Mount seems almost superfluous.[7]

Within this broader movement we can identify what is referred to as the emerging church. The emerging church (with a small "c") is a Christian movement of the late 20th and early 21st centuries. The movement is a response to the perceived influence of modernism in Western Christianity. What those involved in the conversation mostly agree on is their disillusionment with the organized and institutional church. Some core values include desires to imitate the life of Jesus; transform secular society; emphasize communal living; welcome outsiders; be generous and creative; and lead without control.

Three categories are perceived within the movement: Relevants, Reconstructionists, and Revisionists. Relevants are theological conservatives interested in updating to current culture. Reconstructionists are generally theologically evangelical, and speak of new forms of church that result in transformed lives. Revisionists are theologically liberal, and openly question whether evangelical doctrine is appropriate for the postmodern world.

The late theologian and New Testament scholar Marcus Borg (1942-2015) said in 2003 that the emerging paradigm has been visible for well over a hundred years. In the last twenty to thirty years it has become a major grassroots movement among both laity and clergy in "mainline" or "old mainline" Protestant denominations. He described it as a way of seeing the Bible (and the Christian tradition as a whole) as historical, metaphorical and sacramental, and a way of seeing the Christian life as relational and transformational. [8]

This broader movement does not appear to be offering a "new idea of God." But it can be seen as addressing the shrinking purpose of the historical idea of God. It stresses the perfectibility of man today, in the here and now, through the teachings of the pre-Easter Jesus. Isn't this what most mainline churches are doing today (mission), while continuing to emphasize the post-Easter image? This more humanist and inclusive version of Christianity seems to represent a real potential revolution in Christian thinking. (Hold on!)

Some—I believe quite questionably—associate at least the more progressives of the movement with a philosophical movement referred to as the Death of God Theology. This has philosophical roots going back a couple of hundred years, but was sensationalized here in the USA in the mid-1960's (by TIME magazine).[9] While philosophically rational, it so far has failed to gain significant religious traction. But Progressive Christianity seems to have acquired a voice, and even a toehold; perhaps in the twenty-first century, even a foothold.

Looked at historically, perfection does seem today to be the primary remaining relevance of the idea of God left for the Church to concentrate on. Still, an argument can be made that the slide in mainline church attendance took off in the 1970's and was coincident with the full embrace of a variant of Walter Rauschenbusch's turn of the 20th century Social Gospel which emphasized social reform (an aim for perfection) over personal spiritual salvation through Jesus Christ.

As that letter to the editor writer pointed out a bit earlier, the Church needs to be engaged in the world, but in his opinion that's not its primary purpose. And today, many might agree with him. Still, maybe this is today's version and understanding of Matthew 3:1, "Repent, for the kingdom of heaven is near." But if and as this shift to being "more engaged in the world" continues to be the focus of the denominations, I also agree with his observation that such a mission could make God unnecessary and the Church simply a gathering of like-minded individuals.

The Church might take the position that such "good works" are an avenue to the promises of God in the hereafter. But that is going to change the teaching of not just a few that redemption is not earned by good works. As I say, it's going to be a tough transition for most religious folks, no matter which way they jump. Or, don't jump.

Recently I received a letter over the signature of the president of the San Francisco Theological Seminary (SFTS) soliciting funds for a new in-house program called the Center for Innovation in Ministry. STFS is described as an ecumenical Christian graduate school whose mission is to witness to Jesus Christ and to advocate for "social justice" (pretty much the above point about the social gospel in action). The letter explained the purpose of the new center as being to develop new kinds of ministry and new ways to engage the rapidly changing world in which we live; "to bring people together to cultivate fresh approaches to communication …create new possibilities for interaction and develop creative ways to put new ideas to work." The beneficiaries of this new program, according to President McDonald, are all those who are involved in ministry and religious leadership.

To me the letter documents the Church (or at least part of the Church) trying to meet the needs of preparing the clergy to better deal with the religious realities of today. Efforts such as this seem worth supporting (and I did make a contribution). If you read the letter it is pretty clear where they see the efforts the Church needs to make: advocacy for social justice, and the socially needed quest to bring about much-needed spiritual change—more civility, less violence, less injustice. In short, they are working to build a better world. This outreach seems at odds with that letter-to-the-editor writer and more to confirm my stated opinion above that today, and probably for tomorrow, the Church is here and now focused, and primarily on the God-purpose of perfection. I have no argument with that, but as our letter-to-the-editor writer stated, where is the need for God in such an earthly mission? Perhaps it is in the reflection of the perfection of the god of the idea. That certainly works for me.

But at the end of the day, I see the future for today's mainline religious institutions as being tenuous given their current market dynamics and traditional (religious) "business" model. I see it continuing to shrink due to the reduced personal dependence on those three basic human needs that the idea of God traditionally has fulfilled, in spite of ambitious and worthy efforts such as the SFTS's Center for Innovation in Ministry. Unfortunately, to me, those seem like efforts to attack the symptoms and not the basic problem of truth in the context of today. Or, does the Church simply by-pass and ignore the historical message and evolve into just another civic good-works group, call it Progressive or other?

Pity I won't be around to observe the future I foresee, or if wrong, to give people the opportunity to say, we told you so!

Epilogue

Moving On

So, my doubt, my rational resistance to orthodox belief continues, even as my regard for the local church is enhanced by working through this exercise. In my view it isn't really a matter of right or wrong, or true of false. It is a matter, as I said at the beginning, of utility, of satisfying needs. Back in Chapter Four I made reference to the saying (Voltaire's, I believe) that if the Church didn't exist, someone would have to invent it, or words to that effect. I also quoted rabbi Jonathan Sacks who said recently, "No society has survived for long without either a religion or a substitute for religion." Likewise I raised the question, is the non-material need (spirituality) of humanity today meaningful? The real question is, why is it necessary? What is it that we—you and I—really need from a religion? So, as I seek this understanding for myself, I trust you will pursue belief as you determine most appropriate for you and your circumstances. It's your choice, of course, but I recommend you not sell Christianity's message short, at least not yet.

One rather unexpected result of my inquiry here is I believe I have uncovered my own religious ideology. I'm a somewhat freethinking Christian religious liberal; one with rational humanist sympathies (Oh dear!). Given my comments throughout this polemic, that now seems pretty evident. Need I apologize? For what, to whom? I think not. I have already admitted to discarding the cloak of skepticism.

And consider that I am what I am is due in at least some part to the influence and teaching of the Church itself. Must it not bear some responsibility for the result of my—and others'—present religious ambivalence and doubt? Still, there may be hope for me. How so? Well, I try to follow the advice of a placard that sits in my office: *You never fail until you stop trying.* So I'm still trying, and I want to believe the Church is too.

I began this polemic stating that my message, be it what it is, is intended for the Church. It is, admittedly, a somewhat critical and non-orthodox analysis in numerous aspects, but hopefully provided in a positive and helpful manner as is intended. I have documented numerous others' critical comments/observations such to suggest my thoughts here are neither irrational nor unique. I highlighted theologian Karl Barth's suggestion that the most pressing question people ask when hearing a sermon is, "Is it true?" That equates to doubt; doubt leads to all kinds of other questions which, in the end, if not satisfactorily and rationally answered leads to more doubt. It's a vicious downward spiral resulting too often in a loss of faith. And faith is what religion is about. That seems such an obvious statement. Still, I guess you have to consider its lay source.

I'm neither so naïve nor egotistical to believe that my layman's story will in and of its own alter the direction of the mainline church (Imagine a row boat trying to turn the direction of a superliner under way; yeah!). My hope is it might empower others who likewise harbor doubt to speak out. Certainly as we've seen, enough seem to be voting with their feet. While this obviously concerns the Church I continue to theorize that the Church believes it is not responsible for this exodus from religious life. Maybe it's not. Maybe today there is just that much more clamoring for our attention that what the Church has to competitively offer for our time and attention is not compelling. But either way, the end effect seems the same.

I come back to Karen Armstrong's observation in the final chapter of her 1993 book *A History of God*: "How will the idea of God survive in the years to come? For 4000 years it has constantly adapted to meet the demands of the present, but in our own century, more and more people have found that it no longer works for them, and when religious ideas cease to be effective, they fade away."[1] Just who do we look to to keep this indispensably necessary idea of God alive, if not to the Church?

In spite of my rather pessimistic comments in the last chapter, today we still have a fairly vibrant religious community—almost everywhere. It's not monolithic, it's not always united in its views and divine teachings. Nevertheless, it is! The Christian Church here in the West is struggling in several areas as I (and others) have pointed out. The relationship between science and religion—between reason and revelation—has been since classical times, and increasingly so for the past few centuries, a significant issue to come to grips with. In Chapter Five we raised the Galileo/Church conflict as a prime example. I mentioned that in 1992 (October 31st to be exact), then Pope John Paul II gave a speech entitled (in English) *Faith Can Never Conflict with Reason* that appeared to exonerate Galileo, even chide the clergy, just a bit.

Following the Vatican II conclave, in 1979 Pope John Paul II expressed that he wished that the Pontifical Academy of Sciences would conduct an in-depth study of the celebrated and controversial "Galileo Case." A commission was established in 1981, and on that Saturday morning 31 October 1992 they presented their conclusions to the Pope in the Sala Regia of the Apostolic Palace. In his remarks thanking the Commission—delivered in French to a wide audience of the Pontifical Academy, heads of the diplomatic missions accredited to the Holy See, and other dignitaries, the Pope addressed the general issue of science versus theology. I won't ask you to sit through his entire speech, but do believe the following two paragraphs of English translation are enlightening and relevant to my story here:

Humanity has before it two modes of development. The first involves culture, scientific research and technology. That is to say whatever falls within the horizontal aspect of man and creation which is growing at an impressive rate. In order that this progress should not remain completely external to man, it presupposes a simultaneous raising of conscious, as well as its activation. The second mode of development involves what is deepest in the human being, when transcending the world and transcending himself, man turns to the One who is the Creator of all. It is only this vertical direction which can give full meaning to man's being and action, because it situates him in relation to his origin and his end. In this twofold direction, horizontal and vertical, man realizes himself fully as a spiritual being and as Homo sapiens. But we see that development is not uniform and linear, and that progress is not always well ordered. This reveals the disorder which affects the human condition. The scientist who conscious of this twofold development and takes it into account contributes to the restoration of harmony.

Those who engage in scientific and technological research admit as the premise of its progress, that the world is not a chaos but a "cosmos" – that is to say that there exists order and natural laws which can be grasped and examined and which for this reason, have a certain affinity with the spirit. Einstein used to say: "What is eternally incomprehensible in the world is that it is comprehensible." This intelligibility, attested to by the marvelous discoveries of science and technology leads us, in the last analysis, to that transcendent and Primordial Thought imprinted upon all things."

Some might call this stonewalling by the Pope. To me, this appears as a not unreasonable attempt on the part of the Church to harmonize the scientific with the theological, giving credit to the scientific where credit is due, or at least cannot be denied, while maintaining my point made earlier that man has a need for a non-material side of life. As his Holiness put it, a vertical aspect of humanity; a balance of kind of the what (science) with the why (the Church). Truthfully, it's not a point I would care to have to defend too strongly, at least as he made it. Nonetheless, it seems a valid point, presenting a human need, as I hope I have demonstrated.

The other point that I believe the Holy Father made in support of my thesis here is his reference in his final sentence to the "Thought" (with a capital T), that "transcendent and Primordial Thought." Note that not here, nor elsewhere in his remarks to the Academy, did he mention God. But I believe he just endorsed my expressed belief that it is the Thought, the idea of God, which is the crucial matter in man's faith.

I believe in that idea of God. My personal dilemma is that I simply cannot presently unconditionally support the Western Christian vision of the god of the idea today, as I none the less honestly pass the Peace of Christ on Sunday mornings in church. After all…it's the idea that counts! I trust that you are not likewise conflicted.

As I exit stage-left here, I ask you to think about it: THE IDEA OF GOD. Think devoutly about it. It makes little difference, really, how you opt to observe it. Nor whether you are passionate, just casual or even skeptical in your thinking about it. Recognize what it has provided us with, personally and beyond. Respect it and respect the religious institutions that protect and promote it. It's not only a good idea, when properly embraced, it's most likely the best idea we have ever had. In this connection, I leave you with some sound advice:

"If a man does away with his traditional way of living and throws away his good customs, he had better first make certain that he has something of value to replace them."[2]

TRH May 2017

Appendix A

An Example of the Problem of Change

Such a reduced depicted dependence on a shrinking Church leaves hanging that apparent non-material side of humanity. What about that? Does man simply go the materialistic way? I doubt it. Why not, considering the above comments, i.e., the perceived need here for less and less personal "spiritual" guidance? Because it just doesn't seem to be in our nature to be so one dimensional, especially in the area of "perfection." But for the Church to continue to be looked to as a necessary source of support for this perceived need, things are going to have to happen.

The Church will probably have to review its message, its mission, and its focus; in short its purpose—not just its communication skills. We pointed out earlier that Christianity is not monolithic. But today it seems the Church is beset increasingly with conflict and even strife as the result of cultural changes. How did that old commercial put it: This is not your father's Oldsmobile! Unfortunately, and for better or worse, the Church today still is in most relevant aspects your father's (and grandfather's and great grandfather's) model under the hood. Even very little cosmetic changes. A one size fits all religious approach seems hard to sell today.

Conservative and Progressive Christians have different images of God; the meaning of Jesus, what happened on the Cross, the nature of sin, and the origins of life. They differ on how to interpret scripture, what it means to be "saved," their notions of heaven and hell, and what is meant by "the end."

Is it its mission simply to competitively increase the numbers of people who "come to (its) God"; "come to Jesus," come to be "saved" from their sinful (dark) side? My bet would be that this double-edged message of salvation (or else!) is going to be of limited value to keeping let alone increasing church membership. My layman's speculation is that it will probably be more productive for the Church and beneficial for the community if the Church "sells" (emphasizes) perfection and downplays its sin based consideration of salvation. While the two might not be mutually exclusive, it's the carrot of salvation (or not) that I would suggest is a probable turn-off marketing approach in this day and age, especially among the younger among us who stand to make up the future of the Church.

This also does not say churches will disappear like buggy-whip makers, even if physically many seem destined to do. Example: In the U.S. Southern Baptist Convention a recent report showed that 1,000 churches a year disappear from the denomination's data base. It did not indicate just how many new ones were added a year. [1] Again, no society has succeeded for long without religion, or a substitute for religion. There is certainly a need today, and will probably be one in a hundred years for a non-material side of humanity. I foresee the church of today (and yesterday) morphing into a substitute for or at least a modification of religion for tomorrow. It will be one that emphasizes the "perfection" idea. An ethical and moral backbone for society with, for those few, a continued if de-emphasized divine sub-menu. It's easy to write about this, theoretically, but it is going to take wrenching change within the Church. It may even not be possible to pull off, internally. Let me give you some idea of the difficulty here.

In a recent essay in the publication *The Atlantic* (May 2015,) The New York Times columnist Ross Douthat—himself a Catholic—highlighted just how difficult effecting change, and especially doctrinal change, in the Church will be. He based his argument on recent actions of Pope Francis and his apparent desire to see and direct such change. For example, explains Douthat:

Francis has officially reaffirmed Church teaching on sex and marriage, as he has shown persistent impatience with the obstacle these teachings present to bringing some lapsed Catholics back to the Church. On the issue of divorce and remarriage, the Pope seems to be tacitly supportive of the idea to allow Catholics in a second marriage to receive communion even if their first marriage is still considered (by the Church) valid. That is, even if they are living in what the Church considers an adulterous relationship.

Independent of just how this might be authorized, formally by the Vatican or informally at the local level, it has inevitable doctrinal implications. If people who are living as adulterers can receive Communion, if the Church can recognize their state of life as non-ideal but somehow tolerable, then either the Church's sacramental theology or its definition of sin has been effectively rewritten. The ramifications of such a change are potentially sweeping. If ongoing adultery is forgivable, then why not other forms of loving, long-standing sexual commitment? Not only same-sex couples but cohabiting straight couples and even polygamous families (a particular concern among African cardinals) could make a plausible case that they deserve the same pastoral exception, rendering the very idea of objective sexual sin anachronistic in one swift march—the so called slippery slope; where does it end?

Altering a teaching that the Church has spent centuries insisting it simply cannot alter is a very difficult thing. But getting around it, side-stepping it in the end, perhaps not impossible. In this specific case Pope Francis is not messing with the teaching of the Church. He is messing with the Church's annulment law by radically reforming the annulment process to make the decrees easier to obtain. Canon lawyers and conservatives have balked at the new law, asserting that it amounts to "Catholic divorce," a charge Francis has vigorously denied. Will it effectively introduce change without apparent change of doctrine? Maybe, if obtaining annulments becomes as easy as applying. The problem one can foresee in such an end-around tactic is that, given enough of them, the credulity of the Church's doctrines and teachings lose their ethical and moral significance.

While we have been speaking above specifically regarding the Roman Catholic Church, the same observations are applicable generally. We have already seen signs of stress in several of the Protestant denominations over the current cultural issues surrounding sex, both within and without the institutions themselves.

No, internal change will not come easily nor without strong resistance. No religion, like no democracy, is monolithic. Given enough reasons and frictions, schisms will occur. But history is full of such doctrinal separations, going back to the East-West split into Roman and Eastern Orthodox Church blocs. Maybe that is a sign of "progress" in itself, and is not only to be expected, but encouraged. Why so? Because it at least potentially offers more choice (satisfaction) to more people as to what and how they believe in the god of the idea, and even to how they may express their belief. In this sense, religion like society in general is in somewhat of a constant mode of progress, or at least what I categorize as progress. This does, you have to admit, make looking forward a hundred years somewhat murky.

What do you think?

About the Author

With more than 35 years of lay religious experience and exposure at the local church level, the author has become increasingly concerned—as others no doubt have—about the Christian church's present health and future role within society. History suggests that societies benefits from a supporting and healthy religious community. Convinced that its "professionals" need to hear from the concerned thousands sitting in the pews, he writes as one of them and suggests a collective voice.

Thomas Richard Harry, "TR", and his wife live in Windsor, California. Writing, while not his vocation, is his avocation.

Notes

Prologue: God and Me, A Shaky Relationship at Best

1   Quoted by Peter W. Marty in "From the Publisher" *The Christian Century*, 5/10/17, p. 3

2   By definition in a religious context, a layman, or layperson, is a non-ordained member of the church. In some instances, laypersons with or without specialized training may work in close rapport with the clergy in both the teachings, preaching and administration of the church. My usage of the term "layman" does not exclude such but is more broadly intended to apply to the general laity; parishioner or congregant, those most usually sitting in the pews come Sunday mornings. Those who until recently primarily saw their role in the church being to "pray, pay and obey" as I have heard it put.

3   Wikipedia.org/anselm_of_canterbury

Chapter One: A Steep Hill To Climb

1   The USA's National Academy of Science supports the view that science and religion are independent. Science and religion are based on different aspects of human experience. In science, explanations must be based on evidence drawn from examining the natural world. Scientifically based observations or experiments that conflict with an explanation eventually must lead to modification or even abandonment of that explanation. Religious faith, in contrast, does not depend on empirical evidence, is not necessarily modified in the face of conflicting evidence, and typically involves supernatural forces or entities. Because they are not a part of nature, supernatural entities cannot be investigated by science. In this sense, science and religion are separate and address aspects of human understanding in different ways.

Chapter Two: Looking Back to Look Ahead

1   *Matthew* 3:17, The New International Version (NIV) Study Bible (Grand Rapids Zondervan Bible Publishers 1985)
2   *Exodus* 18: 14-17, NIV Study Bible
3   *Exodus:* Chapters 18-23, NIV Study Bible
4   Ronàld Hendel, *The Book of Genesis, a Biography* (Princeton & Oxford, Princeton University Press 2013)

Chapter Three: The Church's Story

1   Karen Armstrong, *A History of God* (New York, Ballantine Books 1993), p. 345
2   Armstrong, *A History of God*, p. 350
3   Armstrong, *A History of God*, p. 352
4   *Matthew* 5:22, 41, 46; *Luke* 16:23, NIV Study Bible
5   *Matthew* 4:17, NIV Study Bible
6   *The Christian Century*, 1/30/2016 (Chicago), Letters to the Editor
7   Armstrong, *A History of God*, p. 129
8   *Romans* 3:22-24, NIV Study Bible
9   Kay Arthur, *"Lord, I need grace to make it"* (Sisters, Oregon Questar Publishing Family 1989), p. 21
10 www.explorefaith.com
11 *Ephesians* 2:8-10, NIV Study Bible
12 *John* 1:17, NIV Study Bible
13 *Encyclopedia Britannica (*on-line*); Paul Tillich, American Theologian and Philosopher*

Chapter Four: The Church's Story II

1   *Introduction to the Book of Ecclesiastes*, NIV Study Bible
2   *Matthew* 19:30, NIV Study Bible
3   *Acts* 13:38, NIV Study Bible
4   Book review quote of John Casey's *"After Lives, a Guide to Heaven, Hell and Purgatory"* (New York Wall Street Journal 10/24/09), p. W-11
5   *John* 11:26-27, NIV Study Bible
6   Fewer churches, www.pathos.com/thechristiancrier
7   *The Christian Century*, 2/14/15, p.
8   Robin R. Meyers, *Saving Jesus From the Church* (San Francisco HarperOne), p. 77

9   Clement of Alexandria (c. 150CE – c. 215CE) believed that "the idea of God" was implanted in man's soul in the form of a spark kindled by the divine *Logos*. See Geza Vermes, *Christian Beginnings* (Yale University Press 2013), p. 211)

Chapter Five: Religious Reality: God vs. The Idea of God

1   Quoted from Michael Lacewing's *The Idea of God* at alevelphilosophy.co.uk, the Routledge Taylor & Francis Group
2   Quoted from Network monitoring tool, www.budas.org
3   Albert Einstein: *The idea of God is a "product of human weakness," the bible "pretty childish"* (Rationalist International.net/article/2008)
4   From Wikipedia, the free encyclopedia, www.en.wikipedia.org/wiki/Reality
5   Quoted from Michael Lacewing's *The Idea of God*
6   There are those who would say I am not talking about God (with a capital G) at all here, simply a god (small g)—call it a demiurge—that may have created the material universe, but is not the transcendent divine responsible for all contingent being.
7   Michael Polanyi, *Science Faith and Society* (Chicago & London, The University of Chicago Press 1964)
8   From Wikipedia, the free encyclopedia, www.wikipedia.com, Roman church C.D.F.
9   From Wikipedia, the free encyclopedia, www.wikipedia.com, Jacques Dupuis
10   One fine example is the prolific writer and teacher David Bentley Hart in his 2013 book, *The Experience of God: Being, Consciousness, Bliss.* Hart, an Orthodox Christian philosophical theologian, lately a Templeton Fellow at Norte Dame's Institute for Advanced Study, argues aggressively against accepting the worldly atheistic (or scientific/materialistic) explanation of reality as conclusive, or certainly as final. Full disclosure: At the time of writing this I had not yet finished reading this book, but can attest that the first almost one hundred pages of this three hundred thirty-two page book is devoted to this end. I continued to read it with much interest in as much as being Orthodox in his theology, I expected to hear the god of the idea expressed in terms not common among most Western mainline Christian writers. I wasn't disappointed.
11   Hendel, *The Book of Genesis*, p. 61
12   *The Christian Century*, 2/4/2015, 7/8/2015
13   *The Christian Century*, 12/9/2015
14   *Joseph Campbell and the Power of Myth*, six program video series w/Bill Moyers (apostrophe S. Publications, Inc. 1988)
15   *The Christian Century*, 6/10/2015

16 Armstrong, *A History of God*, p. 377
17 *The Christian Century,* 5/27/2015
18 Armstrong, *A History of God*, p. 104
19 *Who Is the Pope?* (New York Review of Books 2/19/2015), p. 12
20 Armstrong, *A History of God*, p. 389
21 *The Christian Century,* 3/30/2016, p. 10
22 Armstrong, *A History of God*, p. 312
23 While I accept responsibility for the conclusion I draw here, I can't and don't take credit (or blame) for originating this rather remarkable assertion. The idea that religion is not something instituted by God, but rather is man-made, can be traced back to ancient Greece. In the eighteenth century, it began to seem possible to finally substantiate what had previously been mere speculation. Ludwig Feuerbach, a German theorist of religion, drawing upon Hegelian philosophy, set out the idea that the process by which religion was invented was wish fulfillment. God, according to Feuerbach, is a projection of the strongest desires of humanity. This seems consistent with the conclusions reached here in Chapter Five and, we will see, in Chapter Six as well.

Chapter Six: The Purpose of God

1 *Titus* 2: 11-14; *1 John* 3:3, NIV Study Bible
2 *Romans* 8:24-25; *Hebrews* 11: 1-7, NIV Study Bible
3 *Ecclesiastes* 11:5, NIV Study Bible
4 In psychology, cognitive dissonance is the mental stress or discomfort experienced by an individual who holds two or more contradictory beliefs, ideas or values at the same time, performs an action that is contrary to one or more beliefs, ideas, or values, or is confronted by new information that conflicts with existing beliefs, ideas or values. (www.en.wikipedia.org/cognative dissonance)
5 Basic humanism is an outlook or system of thought attaching prime importance to human rather than divine or supernatural matters. Humanist beliefs stress the potential value and goodness of human beings, emphasize common human needs, and seek solely rational ways of solving human problems. (www.en.wikipedia.org/wiki/humanism)

Chapter Seven: The Jesus Phenomenon

1 *Mark* 1:11, NIV Study Bible
2 *Matthew* 3:17, NIV Study Bible
3 Geza Vermes, *Christian Beginnings* (Yale University press 2012) p. 29
4 Vermes, *Christian Beginnings*, p. 29

5   Geza Vermes, *The Authentic Gospel of Jesus* (Penguin Books 2004) p. 398

6   *Mark* 7:27; *Matthew* 15:26, 10:5-8, NIV Study Bible

7   *Romans* 1:4, NIV Study Bible

8   John Shelby Spong, *Why Christianity Must Change or Die* (HarperOne 1999) pp. 73-80

9   Rival Telling, *Shared Stories*, The Christian Century 8/19/2015

10 Alan Jacobs, *Original Sin* (HarperOne 2008) p. 4, 11-14

11 Jacobs *Original Sin*, p. 108

12 Wikipedia.org

13 *The Christian Century*, 3/20/2013

14 Vermes, *The Authentic Gospel of Jesus*, p. 390

15 Vermes, whom I call upon throughout this chapter, was considered by some as one of the world's greatest experts on early Christianity, and the Dead Sea Scrolls. He passed away in 2015.

16 Vermes, *Christian Beginnings*, pp. 223-227

17 Armstrong, *A History of God*, p. 107

18 Karen Armstrong, *The Bible, a Biography* (New York Grove Press 2007), p. 118

19 See for example Spong, *Why Christianity Must Change or Die*, and Meyers, *Saving Jesus from the Church.*

20 NIV Study Bible

21 St. Augustine, "on the Trinity, xiii," quoted in Armstrong, *A History of God*, p. 123

22 *The Christian Century*, 1/20/2016, p. 9

23 Vermes, *Christian Beginnings*, pp. 235-236

24 Vermes, *Christian Beginnings*, pp. 60, 237

25 Vermes, *Christian Beginnings*, p. 234

26 Vermes, *Christian Beginnings*, p. 234

27 Armstrong, *A History of God*, p. 114

28 Armstrong, *A History of God*, p. 117

Chapter Eight: Does Jesus Equal God?

1   Huston Smith, *The World's Religions* (Harper San Francisco, 1991) pp 340-343

2   David Bentley Hart, *The Experience of God, Being, Consciousness, Bliss* (Yale University Press 2013) p. 135-136

3   Bertrand Russell, *Why I Am Not a Christian* (Touchstone Books, 1957 by George Allen & Unwin Ltd.), p. 30

Chapter Nine: Picking a Path: The church's Continuing Role Providing for Man's Non-Material Needs

1   The Public Square, by R.R. Reno, *First Things Magazine* May 2017, p. 67
2   *Genesis* 9: 12-17, NIV Study Bible
3   Joseph Bottum, quoted in "That New Time Religion," *Claremont Review of Books*, Summer 2015, p. 15
4   Catholicism in an Age of Discontent, by Thomas J. White, *First Things Magazine* November 2016, p. 26.
5   The End of Christendom, by Eamon Duffy, *First Things Magazine* November 2016, p. 52, 57.
6   Armstrong, *A History of God,* p. 389
7   Meyers, *Saving Jesus From the Church*, p. 7, 19
8   Emerging church, www.wikipedia.org
9   Matthew Rose, "Death of God Fifty Years On," *First Things Magazine* August/September 2016, p. 43

Epilogue: Moving On

1   Armstrong, *A History of God*, p 37
2   Old Bantu proverb quoted by Robert Ruark in his 1955 novel *Something of Value*

Appendix A: An Example of the Problem of Change

1   *The Christian Century*, 3/30/2016, p. 14

Bibliography

The NIV Study Bible (Grand Rapids, MI., Zondervan Bible Publishers, 1985)

The Layman's Parallel Bible, comparing the King James version, the Modern Language Bible, the Living Bible, the Revised Standard Version (Zondervan)

The Books of The Bible, New Testament NIV Version (Colorado Springs, Biblica, Inc. 2011)

Karin Armstrong, *A History of God* (New York, Ballantine Books, 1993)

Karin Armstrong, *The Bible, a Biography* (New York, Grove Press, 2007)

Harold Bloom, *Jesus and Yahweh, the Names Divine* (New York, Riverhead Books 2005)

Harold Bloom, *The American Religion* (New York, Chu Hartley Publishers, 2006)

Raymond E. Brown, *An Introduction to the NEW TESTAMENT* (New York, Doubleday, 1997)

The Dead Sea Scrolls, A New Translation, by M.O. Wise, M.G. Abegg Jr., & E.M. Cook (San Francisco, Harper, 2005)

John Patrick Diggins, *Why Niebuhr Now?* (Chicago & London, The University of Chicago Press, 2011)

The Ecclesiastical History of EUSEBIUS PAMPHILUS, Bishop of Cesarea, translated from the original with an Introduction by Christian Frederick Cruse and Historical View of The Council of

Nice by Isaac Boyle (Grand Rapids, Michigan, Baker Book House, 1969)

David Bentley Hart, *The Experience of GOD, Being, Consciousness, Bliss* (Yale University Press, 2013)

Ronald Hendel, *The Book of Genesis, A Biography* (Princeton and Oxford Princeton University Press, 2013)

Alan Jacobs, *Original SIN, A Cultural History* (New York, HarperOne, 2008)

Christopher Knight & Robert Lomas, *The Hiram Key* (New York, Barnes & Noble Books, 1998)

C.S. Lewis, *Mere Christianity* (San Francisco, HarperOne, 1952 and 2001)

Mario Livio, *Is GOD a Mathematician?* (New York, London, Simon & Schuster, 2009)

Donald K. McKim, *Westminster Dictionary of Theological Terms* (Louisville & London, Westminster, John Knox Press, 1996)

John Mickelthwait & Adrian Wooldridge, *GOD IS BACK* (New York, The Penguin Press, 2009)

Robin R. Meyers, *Saving Jesus from the Church* (New York, HarperOne, 2009)

Reinhold Niebuhr, *Major Works on Religion and Politics*, Elisabeth Sifton, editor (New York, The Library of America, 2015)

Elaine Pagels, *Beyond Belief, The Secret Gospel of Thomas* (New York, Vintage Books, 2004)

Michael Polanyi, *Science, Faith and Society* (Chicago & London, University of Chicago Press, 1964)

Sandra L. Richter, *The EPIC of EDEN, A Christian Entry into the Old Testament* (Downers Grove, Illinois, IVP Academic, 2008)

Thomas Römer, *The Invention of God*, translated by Raymond Geuss (London, Harvard University Press, 2015)

Bertrand Russell, *Why I Am Not a Christian and other essays on religion and related subjects* edited by Paul Edwards (Touchstone Books, 1957)

E. P. Sanders, *The Historical Figure of JESUS* (New York & London, Penguin Books, 1993)

John Shelby Spong, *Why Christianity Must Change or Die* (New York, HarperOne, 1998)

James D. Tabor, *PAUL AND JESUS, How the Apostle Transformed Christianity* (New York, Simon & Schuster Paperbacks, 2013)

Geza Vermes, *Christian Beginnings, From Nazareth to Nicaea* (New Haven & London, Yale University Press, 2012)

Geza Vermes, *The Authentic Gospel of JESUS* (London & New York, Penguin Books, 2004)

A.J. Wallace & R.D. Rusk, *Moral Transformation, The Original Christian Paradigm of Salvation* (New Zealand, Bridgehead Publishing, 2011)

Jim Wallis, *On God's Side* (Grand Rapids, Michigan Brazos Press, 2013)

Jim Wallis, *The Great Awakening* (New York, HarperOne, 2008)

Garry Wills, *What the Gospels Meant* (New York, Viking Penguin, 2008)

Garry Wills, *Head and Heart, American Christianities* (New York, The Penguin Press, 2007)

Printed in the United States
By Bookmasters